Mrs. Claus Shares Stories From the Heart

Compiled and Edited by

Jeanetta Bearden Pollard

Success Ranch Publishers

07

Success Ranch Publishers
Boaz, Kentucky   42027-0007

Foreword

Jeanetta Pollard has gathered a series of stories using Biblical principles to teach lessons for life. These are stories of hope and inspiration, and hope is the necessary ingredient in all of our lives. Encouragement is the fuel on which that hope runs, and this book is full of encouragement.

Mrs. Claus Shares Stories from the Heart is a collection of anecdotes that will bring a lift to the heart and a smile to the lips of the reader. Perfectly formatted for quick, easy reads at momentary intervals, or for an hour's respite from a hectic schedule, it will serve to encourage the reader who needs a boost of inspiration or a moment of reflection.

This little book will make an excellent gift for any occasion and will be a welcome and helpful addition to any library.

Zig Ziglar,
Author *SEE YOU AT THE TOP*

Acknowledgments

I have learned that next to having God in your life, there is nothing more important than family and friends. I have truly been blessed by having many of both, all of whom have been very supportive of my endeavor.

My family has been my main source of inspiration. My husband, Jim, is always my encourager – telling me I can do whatever I want to do. He is my computer adviser whenever I get in trouble, which is often. He and my daughter, Valerie, are my sounding boards. They are used to the question – "What do you think of this?" Valerie also reviewed all the stories for me.

Our son, Barry, who still resides in Fort Lauderdale, Florida, was not here to physically help, but his love and support are always with me.

To Margaret Merrick and Rena Boyd for their proofreading and to Pamela Horne who gave me the idea for the title of the book goes my heart felt thanks. A thanks also goes to Dan Sheppard and Christina Held who assisted with some computer technicalities.

I would like to express my gratitude to the staff of Omni PublishXpress. It has been a pleasure working with Norm Kale and Sue Bryant. Scott Kale did a great job designing the cover.

Last, but certainly not least, are all those who so graciously shared their stories with me; who allowed me the privilege of sharing with you the awe-inspiring things God is doing in their lives. To those whose names are unknown to us, they are known to our Father. He who does things in secret will be rewarded openly. Matthew 6:4

To my Heavenly Father who put this book into my head and my heart long ago, I am grateful I have been able to finish it. Without Him, I could do nothing. He has been my guiding force in this as He has been in all my life.

The Introduction

Being married for over 40 years to a man who is both Santa Claus and a minister has earned me the title of Mrs. Claus. It has also allowed me the privilege of seeing God's hand moving in the lives of both adults and children.

The purpose of my book is to show what God is doing in people's lives today. I have received stories from business people, professors, ministers, teachers and just *plain folk*. My stories have come from personal contacts, newspapers, mail, Internet and magazines. They made me laugh; they made me cry. The main thing about the stories is that they all tell the *same* story. God is alive and well today. He is doing things in our lives just as He did in bible days. He loves us no less than He loved those He walked with while He was here on earth. That's exciting news!

I hope your heart will be touched just as mine was. If it is, then my purpose for this project will have been well served.

Contents

Tell Them for Me

Some twelve years ago, I stood watching my university students file into the classroom for our first session in the Theology of Faith. That was the first day I saw Tommy.

My eyes and my mind both blinked. He was combing his long flaxen hair, which hung six inches below his shoulders. It was the first time I had ever seen a boy with hair that long. I guess it was just coming into fashion then. I know in my mind that it isn't what's on your head but what's in it that counts; but on that day I was unprepared and my emotions flipped. I immediately filed Tommy under "S" for strange… *very strange*.

Tommy turned out to be the "atheist in residence" in my Theology of Faith course. He constantly objected to, smirked at or whined about the possibility of an unconditionally loving Father/God. We lived with each other in relative peace for one semester, although I admit he was, for me at times, a serious pain in the back pew.

When he came up at the end of the course to turn in

his final exam, he asked in a slightly cynical tone, "Do you think I'll ever find God?" I decided instantly on a little shock therapy. "No!" I said very emphatically. "Oh," he responded, "I thought that was the product you were pushing."

I let him get five steps from the classroom door and then called out, "Tommy! I don't think you'll ever find Him, but I am *absolutely certain* that He will find you!"

He shrugged a little and left my class and my life.

I felt slightly disappointed at the thought that he had missed my clever line, "He will find you!" At least I thought it was clever. Later, I heard that Tommy had graduated, and I was duly grateful.

Then a sad report. I heard that Tommy had terminal cancer. Before I could search him out, he came to see me. When he walked into my office, his body was very badly wasted, and the long hair had all fallen out as a result of chemotherapy. But his eyes were bright and his voice was firm, for the first time.

"Tommy, I've thought about you so often. I hear you are sick." I blurted out.

"Oh, yes, very sick. I have cancer in both lungs. It's a matter of weeks."

"Can you talk about it, Tom?" I asked.

"Sure, what would you like to know?" he replied.

"What's it like to be only twenty-four and dying?"

"Well, it could be worse."

"Like what?"

"Well, like being fifty and having no values or ideals, like being fifty and thinking that booze, seducing women and making money are the real "biggies" in life."

I began to look through my mental file cabinet under

"S" where I had filed Tommy as strange. (It seems as though everybody I try to reject by classification, God sends back into my life to educate me.)

"But what I really came to see you about," Tom said, "is something you said to me on the last day of class." (He remembered!) He continued, "I asked you if you thought I would ever find God and you said, 'No!' which surprised me. Then you said, 'But He will find you.' I thought about that a lot, even though my search for God was hardly intense at that time. (My "clever" line. He thought about that a lot!) But when the doctors removed a lump from my groin and told me that it was malignant, then I got serious about locating God. And when the malignancy spread into my vital organs, I really began banging bloody fists against the bronze doors of heaven. But God did not come out. In fact, nothing happened. Did you ever try anything for a long time with great effort and with no success? You get psychologically glutted, fed up with trying. And then you quit. Well, one day I woke up, and instead of throwing a few more futile appeals over that high brick wall to a God who may be or may not be there, I just quit. I decided that I didn't really care...about God, about an afterlife, or anything like that. I decided to spend what time I had left doing something more profitable. I thought about you and your class and I remembered something else you had said:

'The essential sadness is to go through life without loving. But it would be almost equally sad to go through life and leave this world without ever telling those you loved that you had loved them.'

'So, I began with the hardest one, my dad. He was reading the newspaper when I approached him.'

'Dad...'

'Yes, what?' he asked without lowering the newspaper.

'Dad, I would like to talk with you.'

'Well, talk.'

'I mean…it's really important.'

The newspaper came down three slow inches. 'What is it?'

'Dad, I love you. I just wanted you to know that.'"

Tom smiled at me and said with obvious satisfaction, as though he felt a warm and secret joy flowing inside of him.

"The newspaper fluttered to the floor. Then my father did two things I could never remember him ever doing before. He cried and he hugged me. And we talked all night, even though he had to go work the next morning. It felt so good to be close to my father, to see his tears, to feel his hug, to hear him say that he loved me.

"It was easier with my mother and little brother. They cried with me, too, and we hugged each other, and started saying nice things to each other. We shared the things we had been keeping secret for so many years. I was only sorry about one thing: that I had waited so long.

"Here I was, just beginning to open up to all the people I had actually been close to. Then, one day I turned around and God was there. He didn't come to me when I pleaded with Him. I guess I was like an animal trainer holding out a hoop, 'C'mon, jump through.' 'C'mon, I'll give you three days, three weeks.' Apparently God does things in His own way and at His own hour. But the important thing is that He was there. He found me. You were right. He found me even after I stopped looking for Him."

"Tommy," I practically gasped, "I think you are saying something very important and much more universal than you realize. To me, at least, you are saying that the surest way to find God is not to make him a private possession, a problem solver, or an instant consolation in time of need, but rather by opening to love. You know, the Apostle John said that. He said: 'God is love, and anyone who lives in love is living with God and God is living in Him.'"

"Tom, could I ask you a favor? You know, when I had you in class, you were a real pain. But (laughingly) you can make it all up to me now. Would you come into my present Theology of Faith course and tell them what you have just told me? If I told them the same thing it wouldn't be half as effective as if you were to tell them."

"Ooh....I was ready for you, but I don't know if I'm ready for your class."

"Tom, think about it. If and when you are ready, give me a call."

In a few days Tom called, said he was ready for the class; that he wanted to do that for God and for me. So we scheduled a date. However, he never made it. He had another appointment, far more important than the one with my class and me.

Of course, his life was not really ended by his death, only changed. He made the great step from faith into vision. He found a life far more beautiful than the eye of man has ever seen or the ear of man has ever heard or the mind of man has ever imagined.

Before he died, we talked one last time. "I'm not going to make it to your class," he said. "I know, Tom." "Will you tell them for me? Will you...tell the whole world for me?"

"I will, Tom. I'll tell them. I'll do my best."

So, to all of you who have been kind enough to hear this simple statement about love, thank you for listening. And to you, Tommy, somewhere in the sunlit, verdant hills of heaven: "I told them, Tommy…as best I could."

John Powell

The Rainstorm

This is a wonderful incident observed by a young man who works for CenturyTel in Monroe, Louisiana, while shopping at Walmart one day.

....she must have been six years old, this beautiful, brown-haired, freckle-faced image of innocence. Her mom looked like someone from the Waltons or a moment captured by Norman Rockwell. Not that she was old-fashioned. Her brown hair was ear-length with enough curl to appear natural. She had on a pair of tan shorts and a light blue knit shirt. Her sneakers were white with a blue trim. She looked like a Mom.

It was pouring rain outside...the kind of rain that gushes over the tops of rain gutters, so much in a hurry to hit the earth it has not time to flow down the spout. Drains in the nearby parking lot were filled to capacity, and some were blocked so that huge puddles formed around parked cars.

We all stood there under the awning and just inside the

door of the Walmart. We waited, some patiently, others irritated because the downpour had messed up their hurried day.

I am always mesmerized by rainfall. I get lost in the sound and sight of the heavens washing away the dirt and dust of the world. Memories of running, splashing so carefree as a child come pouring in as a welcome reprieve from the worries of my day.

Her voice was so sweet as it broke the hypnotic trance in which we were caught. "Mom, let's run through the rain," she said.

"What?" Mom asked.

"Let's run through the rain!" she repeated.

"No, honey. We'll wait until it slows down a bit," Mom replied.

The child waited another minute and repeated her statement. "Mom, let's run through the rain."

"We'll get soaked if we do," Mom said.

"No, we won't, Mom. That's not what you said this morning," the young girl said as she tugged at her mom's arm.

"This morning? When did I say we could run through the rain and not get wet?"

"Don't you remember? When you were talking to Daddy about his cancer, you said, 'If God can get us through this, He can get us through anything!'"

The entire crowd stopped dead silent. You couldn't hear anything but the rain. We all stood silently. No one came or left in the next few minutes.

The mom paused and thought for a moment about what she would say.

Now some would laugh it off and scold her for being

silly. Some might even ignore what was said. But this was a moment of affirmation in a young girl's life, a time when innocent trust can be nurtured so that it will bloom into faith.

"Honey, you are absolutely right. Let's run through the rain. If God let's us get wet, well maybe we just needed washing," the mother said.

Then off they ran. We all stood watching, smiling and laughing as they darted past the cars and yes...through the puddles. They held their shopping bags over their heads just in case. Of course, they got soaked. But a few believers who screamed and laughed like children all the way to their cars, perhaps inspired by their faith and trust, followed them.

I want to believe that somewhere down the road in life this mom will find herself reflecting back on moments they spent together, captured like pictures in the scrapbook of her cherished memories. Maybe when she watches proudly as her daughter graduates; or as her husband walks their daughter down the aisle on her wedding day, she will laugh again. Her heart will beat a little faster. Her smile will tell the world they love each other. But only two people will share that precious moment when they ran through the rain believing that God would get them through.

And yes, I did. I ran. I got wet. I needed washing.

I hope you will also make time to run through the rain.

Author Unknown

Drawn By God

Joe Leatherman was a successful salesman for a food company. He did very well financially. He had a fine house, a wife and two little girls. The problem was he and his wife, Eleanor, could barely stand the sight of each other.

One morning, as they spewed at each other across the breakfast table, Eleanor screamed, "You want to know what I'd like to do? I'll tell you! I'd like to get a divorce."

Her words hit Joe like a kick in the stomach.

For the first time in his life Joe prayed that morning. It went something like this: "Dear God, I'm in an awful mess here with my wife. I love her, and I want a happy home. Please help us get things straightened out. Please help us save our marriage."

A sense of relief came to his heart.

"As I look back," Joe says, "I can understand why I felt a bit of pressure roll off my back. That prayer didn't solve my problem, but it sort of turned the key to start the solution, because when a man asks God for help and when it isn't a selfish prayer but a real desire to know God and do what's right, God is sure to set some wheels in motion."

Joe is right.

God says: *You shall seek me and find me when you shall search for me with your whole heart.*

Here's what happened.

As a salesman Joe reported periodically to an office in Lima, usually coming in on Elida Road, which is U.S. 30. He had noticed construction work on our new plant, but it was of no significance to him. Our STATES SMELTING AND UNITED STATES PLASTIC CORP. lettering was up, but we had not yet installed the CHRIST IS THE ANSWER testimonial.

He didn't know me. He didn't know of my interest in helping men find Christ.

Yet he subsequently told me, "It's a funny thing, I tell you, it was God's doing sure as anything. I'm driving in on U.S. 30 the morning I prayed asking the Lord to help me save my marriage. I come past your plant same as I'd done many times. I see this STATE SMELTING AND UNITED STATES PLASTIC sign. Then all of a sudden it seems like a voice is telling me I should go in and unload my problems to the guy who runs the place. Crazy, huh? I tell you, it made me feel kind of crazy. Well, I wasn't about to make a fool of myself, so I drove by. I mean, how ridiculous could you get—walk into a strange place, ask for a strange man, tell him you and your wife are having a rough time of it?"

Joe decided to forget all about the impulse. Or so he thought!

Things got no better at home.

"I drove past Mr. Tam's place again and again," Joe

tells, "and every time I felt that urge, heard that inner voice. But I couldn't bring myself to go in."

One morning as Joe dressed to report to the office in Lima, a voice seemed to say, "You'll drive by that place again. Are you going to do as I have directed you?"

It seemed ridiculous.

Joe figured if he did stop at our plant, someone would think he had mental problems and call the police.

"Shall I smite you?" a voice seemed to whisper to Joe's thoughts.

At that moment it occurred to him for the first time that this just might be God talking to him. He had prayed. He had asked God for help. Could this possibly be the way God would answer?

So coming in on Route 30 an hour or so later, Joe slowed down, flicked his blinker for a left turn.

But then he ran out of courage.

Turning off the blinker, he accelerated. Only for half a block, however. He had to go back. He didn't know why. He just knew he had to.

When the traffic cleared for a moment, he did a U-turn and drove back toward our plant.

Once again, however, he lost courage and drove on.

But once more he did a U-turn, came back, lost courage, drove, stopped again, turned back.

Finally he drove up to our visitors' parking lot area and came into the office.

"May I help you?" our receptionist asked.

"You sure can," Joe told her. "I want to speak to Mr. States."

"Mr. States?" The girl was taken off-guard a moment.

"The man who owns this place," Joe explained. "Isn't

his name out there on the front?"

"You mean Mr. Tam," the girl said.

She directed him to my office.

After introducing himself, telling me he sold for a large food wholesaler in town, Joe said, "I know you're not in the market for catsup. I'm not here to sell you anything."

I smiled.

"What can I do for you?" I asked.

"Well," Joe hedged a bit, "maybe you'll laugh at me, but I feel God told me to come in here."

I didn't laugh.

"You know anything about our business?" I asked.

"No, sir, I don't."

"I've spoken to several service clubs in the area and in a lot of churches. Have you ever been to a meeting where I was the speaker?"

He shook his head.

"Then did somebody tell you about me?"

No one had.

The reason Joe Leatherman came into my office was because a strong compulsion had come over him. It was the most unprecedented occurrence in all my efforts at personal evangelism.

"I've tried hard enough to avoid coming," he said, "but I knew I had to, so today I did it."

"Tell me why you came."

"I've got a problem."

"What's your problem?"

"Well, I live out there in that new housing area just west of town, and my wife and I have a beautiful place, a couple of nice little girls, but we're in deep trouble."

"In what way?"

"We're about to get divorced, and it tears me up to think about it. I love my wife and our two kids, and I want to hold the home together, but I can't seem to make any headway. I prayed a while back, prayed to God, and as a result, or as near as I can figure, He keeps telling me to come see you."

I took out my Bible and opened it.

"What I need," Joe continued, "is advice on how to get along with my wife."

"No, Joe," I countered, "that isn't what you need."

"It sure is!"

"You need to learn how to get along with Jesus Christ."

Joe braced himself. I knew I had to be careful. He had his mind set on squaring things away with his wife, then going on living the way he had always done.

"Ever read the Bible?" I asked.

"To be real honest," Joe replied, "I've probably not read more than a page of it in my whole lifetime."

So I tried to show Joe God's plan of salvation, but he seemed confused. He told me later that he thought I was trying to induct him into some kind of secret society or an organization in which you learn a set of rules in order to qualify for membership.

I knew I could send him from my office and never see him again. It frightened me, the thought of letting him slip off the hook, and yet I saw we were making no progress.

"Why don't you take a few days to think about what we've talked about?" I suggested. "Then give me a call, and we'll get together and talk some more."

He left.

I bowed my head and prayed for this young man, I

thanked God for sending him to me. I prayed he would come back, see his real need, and let the Holy Spirit show him the answer to that need.

He called several days later. He wanted to talk. He arrived and there was a complete change in his attitude.

"I'd like to talk with you some more about this plan you tried to tell me about," he said.

"God's plan of salvation?"

"That's it."

Joe Leatherman became a new man that day.

Joe's wife questioned her husband's claims at first, wondering if religion might be his last-ditch stand to keep her from leaving. But as the months went by, she saw the change in his life, freedom from old habits, a new love and understanding toward her and the children.

She, too, invited the Son of God into her life.

Dr. Stanley Tam

The Promise of God

Roger Simms walked slowly along the highway. He was lean and hard, physically fit. But he was tired, and the suitcase he carried seemed to grow heavier by the minute. He was anxious to get home, see his parents and his girl and get out of his army uniform once and for all.

A new surge of hope gripped him as another car came into view. With a friendly smile, his thumb went back into the air. The hopes faded, however, when he realized the car coming toward him was a new sleek black Cadillac.

To his surprise, the car stopped and the passenger door opened for him. He ran toward the car and tossed his suitcase into the back seat.

"Thank you!" he said to the stranger inside. "Let me tell you, I appreciate this ride."

"Glad to," the other man responded. "Going home for keeps?"

"You bet!" Roger settled back against the plush seat. "I have never in my whole life been so glad to be going home!"

"Well, you are in luck if you are going to Chicago."

"I am not going quite that far." He hesitated, while his dark eyes roved the beautiful dashboard. "I guess you live in Chicago?"

The other man nodded. "I have a business there. My name is Hanover. Yours?"

"Simms. Roger Simms."

They talked about many things. Cars, sports, business and life in general. They talked about the war and Roger shared some of his experiences with him.

Then, very quietly, the Holy Spirit spoke to Roger's heart, urging him to witness to Mr. Hanover.

"God, I cannot witness to this man about Christ!" he argued silently. "Just look at him! Expensive clothes, fine car, successful business. He would not be interested in spiritual things."

Minutes passed and they chatted some more about impersonal things.

And once more the Spirit of God began to impress Roger to witness to the man who had so kindly given him a ride.

And again Roger rebelled. He could not do that! Why, Mr. Hanover would never listen to conversation about Christ! No, he simply could not do it!

Time passed. In another thirty minutes it would be time for Roger to leave Mr. Hanover. The countryside was flying past—the colorful hues of early spring.

The third time the Holy Spirit began speaking to Roger's heart. Urgently He impressed him to speak to Mr. Hanover about his soul. It was an impression Roger could no longer ignore.

He cleared his throat. "Mr. Hanover, I would like to

talk to you about something very important. I want to talk to you about your soul."

Steel gray eyes pierced Roger's dark ones. But he made no reply.

"Sir, I want you to know that Jesus Christ died on the cross in your place. He loves you beyond human limit."

For the next fifteen minutes Roger poured out his soul. He explained the way of salvation and ultimately asked if Mr. Hanover would not like to receive Christ as his Savior.

To Roger's astonishment, the Cadillac stopped beside the road. He wondered if Mr. Hanover had had enough and was about to dump him. Instead, the businessman bowed his head over the steering wheel of the car and began weeping. Brokenly he wept his way to Christ.

A few minutes later he dropped Roger in front of his house. "Thank you, Roger. This is the greatest thing that has ever happened to me." He fished for his wallet and brought out a small white business card. "This is where you can find me if you are ever in Chicago."

Nothing could compare to his joy, that this day he had won a soul to Christ! Oh, it was great to be home again. The dinner his mother had prepared was wonderful. Spending the evening with his girl was ecstatic. But Mr. Hanover had been born again. That was more important than anything else in the world.

In a few months Roger and Beth were married and in two years a little son was born. He started his own business and God began to bless it.

Then one morning he learned that he must go to Chicago. He dug out a suitcase and began to pack. When he reached into a drawer for some socks, his fingers encountered the small white business card given to him five years before by Mr. Hanover.

A smile lighted Roger's countenance. Why not? He would be right there in the city. Why not look up Mr. Hanover and see how he was getting along?

It was a Tuesday morning. The sting of the first snow was in the air and the steam from various factories hung in the air like great ghostly apparitions. Roger stepped inside the pretentious doors of the Hanover Enterprises.

A receptionist sat at a desk in the plush room before him.

"I am Roger Simms. I would like very much to see Mr. Hanover."

A strange look came over the woman's face. "That is not possible, Mr. Simms."

Roger felt confused. "I am sure he will remember me. I am the hitchhiker he picked up one afternoon five years ago."

The receptionist was unyielding. Then, "Perhaps you would like to talk to Mrs. Hanover?"

Roger was more puzzled than ever. "I don't know Mrs. Hanover, but—-yes, of course, that will be fine." Apparently that was the only way he would find out just what was going on.

A quick message was given over the intercom and then, "Come this way, please, Mr. Simms."

Almost immediately Roger was face to face with a keen-eyed woman in her mid-fifties. She extended her hand. "You knew my husband?"

Roger sat down across from her. "Yes, he picked me up when I was on my way home from the war."

"Can you tell me when that was? I mean, the day?"

Roger thought for a moment before answering. "It was five years ago in the spring. May seventh."

Mrs. Hanover fidgeted. "Please —-did you talk about anything special?" She paused, "What I mean is, how was he that day?"

Roger shrugged and frowned. "Fine. We talked about many things." It was his turn to hesitate. "Mrs. Hanover, I—-we—-talked about spiritual things."

She was incredulous. "SPIRITUAL things?"

"Yes. As a matter of fact, I talked with him about his soul."

Her lips began to tremble. "And? What was his response?"

Roger was more perplexed than ever. But he had come this far so he might as well take the plunge. "Mrs. Hanover, he pulled over to the side of the road and wept against the steering wheel. He gave his life to Christ that day."

Explosive sobs gripped the woman's body. It was as though he had somehow turned a key that had unlocked all her silent agonies.

"I really do not understand what is going on," Roger managed.

Mrs. Hanover tried desperately to get a grip on herself. "I had prayed for my husband's salvation for years," she said at last. "God promised me his salvation."

"And?" Roger probed. "Where is your husband, Mrs. Hanover?"

"He is dead," she wept, struggling with words. "He was in a car crash after he let you out of the car. He—-he never got home. You see, I thought God had not kept His promise." She was sobbing uncontrollably. "I stopped living for God five years ago because I thought He had not kept His word!"

Betty Swinford

The Birdies

Psalms 91:11-12 *"For He will command his angels concerning you to guard you in all your ways; they will lift you up in their hands, so that you will not strike your foot against a stone."*

This is a true story that occurred in 1994 and was told by Lloyd Glen.

Throughout our lives we are blessed with spiritual experiences, some of which are very sacred and confidential, and others, although sacred, are meant to be shared. Last summer my family had a spiritual experience that had a lasting and profound impact on us; one we feel must be shared. It's a message of love. It's a message of regaining perspective, and restoring proper balance and renewing priorities. In humility, I pray that I might, in relating this story, give you a gift my little son, Brian, gave our family one summer day last year.

On July twenty-second I was in route to Washington, DC for a business trip. It was all so very ordinary until we landed in Denver for a plane change. As I collected my belongings from the overhead bin, an announcement was made for Mr. Lloyd Glenn to see the United Customer Service Representative immediately. I thought nothing of it until I reached the door to leave the plane and I heard a gentleman asking every male if he were Mr. Glenn. At this point I knew something was wrong and my heart sunk.

When I got off the plane, a solemn-faced young man came toward me and said, "Mr. Glenn, there is an emergency at your home. I do not know what the emergency is, or who is involved, but I will take you to the phone so you can call the hospital."

My heart was pounding, but the will to be calm took over. Woodenly, I followed this stranger to the distant telephones where I called the number he gave me for the Mission Hospital. My call was put through to the trauma center where I learned that my three-year-old son had been trapped underneath the automatic garage door for several minutes and when my wife had found him, he was dead.

A neighbor who is a doctor had performed CPR and the paramedics had continued the treatment as Brian was transported to the hospital. By the time of my call, Brian was revived and they believed he would live, but they did not know how much damage had been done to his brain, nor to his heart. They explained that the door had completely closed on his little sternum, right over his heart. He had been severely crushed.

After speaking with the medical staff, my wife sounded worried but not hysterical. I took comfort in her calmness. The return flight seemed to last forever, but finally I arrived at the hospital six hours after the garage door had come down. When I walked into the intensive care unit, nothing could have prepared me to see my little son lying so still on a great big bed with tubes and monitors everywhere. He was on a respirator.

I glanced at my wife who stood and tried to give me a reassuring smile. It all seemed like a dream. I was filled in with the details and given a guarded prognosis. Brian was going to live and the preliminary tests indicated that his heart was OK—two miracles, in and of themselves. But only time would tell if his brain received any damage.

Throughout the seemingly endless hours, my wife was calm. She felt that Brian would eventually be all right. I hung on her words and faith like a lifeline. All that night and the next day Brian remained unconscious. It seemed like forever since I had left for my business trip the day before.

Finally at two o'clock that afternoon, our son regained consciousness and sat up uttering the most beautiful words I have ever heard spoken. He said, "Daddy, hold me," and he reached for me with his little arms.

By the next day he was pronounced as having no neurological or physical deficits. The story of his miraculous survival spread throughout the hospital. You cannot imagine our gratitude and joy!

As we took Brian home, we felt a unique reverence for the life and love of our Heavenly Father that comes to those who brush death so closely. In the days that followed there was a special spirit about our home. Our two older children were much closer to their little brother. My wife and I were much closer to each other, and all of us were close as a whole family. Life took on a less stressful pace. Perspective seemed to be more focused, and balance much easier to gain and maintain. We felt deeply blessed. Our gratitude was truly profound.

Almost a month later to the day of the accident, Brian awoke from his afternoon nap and said, "Sit down, Mommy. I have something to tell you."

At this time in his life, Brian usually spoke in small phrases; so to say a large sentence, surprised my wife. She sat down with him on his bed and he began his sacred and remarkable story.

"Do you remember when I got stuck under the garage door? Well, it was so heavy and it hurt really bad. I called to you, but you couldn't hear me. I started to cry, but then it hurt too bad. And then the 'birdies' came."

"The birdies?" my wife asked puzzled.

"Yes," he replied, "'the birdies' made a whooshing sound and flew into the garage. They took care of me."

"They did?"

"Yes," he said, "One of the birdies came and got you. She came to tell you I got stuck under the door."

A sweet reverent feeling filled the room. The spirit was so strong and yet lighter than air. My wife realized that a three-year-old had no concept of death and spirits; so he was referring to the beings that came to him from beyond as "birdies" because they were up in the air like birds that fly.

"What did the birdies look like?" she asked.

Brian answered, "They were so beautiful. They were dressed in white, all white. Some of them had green and white; but some of them had on just white."

"Did they say anything?"

"Yes," he answered. "They told me the baby would be all right."

"The baby?" my wife asked confused.

And Brian answered, "The baby lying on the garage floor." He went on, "You came out and opened the garage door and ran to the baby. You told the baby to stay and not leave."

My wife nearly collapsed upon hearing this; for she had indeed gone and knelt beside Brian's body and seeing his crushed chest and unrecognizable features, knew he was already dead. She looked up around her and whispered, "Don't leave us, Brian, please stay if you can."

As she listened to Brian telling her the words she had spoken, she realized that the spirit had left his body and was looking down from above on this little lifeless form.

"Then what happened?" she asked.

"We went on a trip," he said, "far, far away."

He grew agitated trying to say the things he didn't seem to have the words for. My wife tried to calm and comfort him, and let him know it would be okay. He struggled with wanting to tell something that obviously was very important to him, but finding the words was difficult.

"We flew so fast up in the air. They're so pretty, Mommy," he added.

"And there is lots and lots of 'birdies.'"

My wife was stunned. Into her mind the sweet comforting spirit enveloped her more soundly, but with an urgency she had never before known.

Brian went on to tell her that the "birdies" had told him that he had to come back and tell everyone about the "birdies". He said they brought him back to the house and that a big fire truck, and an ambulance were there. A man was bringing the baby out on a white bed and he tried to tell the man the baby would be okay, but the man couldn't hear him. He said the "birdies" told him he had to go with the ambulance, but they would be near him. He said they were so pretty and so peaceful, and he didn't want to come back.

And then the bright light came. He said that the light was so bright and so warm, and he loved the bright light so much. Someone was in the bright light. Then someone put their arms around him and told him, "I love you but you have to go back. You have to play baseball and tell everyone about the birdies. Then the person in the bright light kissed him and waved bye-bye. Then whoosh, the big sound came and they went into the clouds."

The story went on for an hour. He taught us that "birdies" were always with us, but we don't see them because we look with our eyes and we don't hear them because we listen with our ears. But they are always there; you can only see them in here (he put his hand over his heart). They whisper the things to help us to do what is right because they love us so much.

Brian continued, stating, "I have a plan, Mommy. You have a plan. Daddy has a plan. Everyone has a plan. We must all live our plan and keep our promises. The birdies help us to do that cause they love us so much."

In the weeks that followed, he often came to us and told all, or part of it again and again. Always, the story remained the same. The details were never changed or out of order. A few times he added further bits of information and clarified the message he had already delivered. It never ceased to amaze us how he could tell such detail and speak beyond his ability when he spoke of his "birdies".

Everywhere he went, he told strangers about the "birdies". Surprisingly, no one ever looked at him strangely when he did this. Rather, they always get a softened look on their face and they smile. Needless to say, we have not been the same ever since that day, and I pray we never will be.

Author Unknown

Electrifying Experience Leads Student To School

He wasn't exactly escaping Nineveh. Neither was he a leviathan's lunch. And he wasn't spewed onto the shore like Jonah.

But for Todd Crosby, student at Boyce College in Louisville, Kentucky, 14,400 volts of electricity jolted him into God's will just as effectively.

God's message came around mealtime on a July, 1999 afternoon in South Georgia. Hovering above his cable-laying comrades in an elevated bucket, Crosby considered his lunch options.

But for many weeks, the bivocational pastor and cable television lineman had been prayerfully contemplating more important issues—his future ministerial training. He knew God had called him to Boyce to begin that training.

He just didn't know how he could drop his life, his pastorate and his 40 hour-a-week job and move his family more than 600 miles to Kentucky.

"I kept throwing up so many excuses why I couldn't come here," said Crosby, a Bachelor of Arts student from Baxley, Georgia. "I just felt like there was no way I could pick my family up and move them all the way to Louisville."

"I knew this is what I desired to do," Crosby added. "I guess I'm hard headed. God had to slap me around a little to get me here...He jolted me a little bit."

That jolt came as Crosby pulled up the last span of cable before lunch. Reaching to tie the cable off, he grabbed a line that had entangled with a hot wire 400 feet away.

Without warning, 14,400 volts—seven times more than the voltage used in an electric chair—surged through Crosby. The current blew holes out of his fingers. It traveled through his heart, then his lungs and stomach. Then it exited out his left side, leaving two fist-size holes.

Crosby's charred body clenched so violently his muscles detached from his bones. Somehow he let go of the line. Still conscious, Crosby collapsed in the crate.

"I didn't think I'd ever make it down to the ground," Crosby said.

Not knowing what had happened, his friends lowered him down. His smoking clothes answered their frantic questions.

Far from town or hospitals, the ambulance seemed to take forever to arrive. In those painful minutes, the one Christian in his group prayed over Crosby. "In no time, he had his hands on me and was praying for me," Crosby said. "That could have a lot to do with why I'm still here today."

Rushed to the emergency room and then to the burn

center in Augusta, Georgia, doctors had doubts at first. The pain was excruciating. They could hardly sedate Crosby. And they wondered whether his arm could be salvaged.

But their pessimism soon turned to astonishment. Though he had suffered many burns both inside and outside the skin, most of his vital organs seemed unscathed. The medics marveled. Crosby credits God and the prayers of his family, friends and church.

"It was just a miracle from the word go," Crosby said. "The doctor at the burn center said, 'We see some high voltage [cases], but most of the guys who get what you got never make it to us.'"

After five surgeries, lots of skin grafts and several weeks of recuperation, Crosby experienced a dramatic recovery. "The doctor said, 'Sometimes you just say thank you and go on.' He didn't understand why I was doing as well as I was," Crosby said.

Lying in bed that night, all of Crosby's excuses against coming to Kentucky left him. "I remember the first night laying there in the hospital," Crosby said. "I said, 'Yeah, I get the message now, God.'

I don't know how to put it into words. Once I survived this thing, I knew exactly what I was supposed to do....I know most people who have kind of stared death in the face have said this, but it does make you put things into perspective about what's really important."

Crosby checked out of the hospital within two weeks. Six weeks after the shocking experience, he stepped back into the pulpit. Then last fall he enrolled in Boyce.

"It is a blessing and a privilege to be able to come here and study," Crosby said. "God saved me from this accident. He's made it possible for me to study for a reason. I constantly remind myself of that."

Other than some scars and his testimony, other students would not know of Crosby's incident.

"God is going to put you where he wants you," Crosby said. "I'm living testimony to that. God worked this out from the time I was electrocuted to the time that I got here. He has knocked down one obstacle after another."

Of course, Crosby admits electrocution would not have been his chosen method of correcting his course. But he admits God's method worked. "I just give him the praise and honor and glory for it all because I really shouldn't even be here. From now on, I'll listen a little closer without being so hard headed," Crosby said.

Bryan Cribb

Faith That Couldn't Be Crushed

A Bible League ministry partner told this story of how Christians in North Korea suffered for their faith.

In 1972 the North Korean government was reconstructing a road. They found an old building—half-destroyed during the Korean War, never repaired in nineteen years. When it came time to demolish the building in order to continue the road construction, they found twenty-nine people—all living underground! The people were Christians.

They had not had haircuts, and their faces were pale and like skeletons. Of the twenty-nine, four were children.

The officials gave them an opportunity to deny their faith, but none of the group would. The officials put the four children under trees, ready to be hanged, and gave them one more chance. But the mother of one child stepped close and told them all, "Go home in peace. We'll be joining you in a few minutes." The children died.

The officials tried again to persuade the Christians. "We'll give you clothes, land, jobs, and homes," they said, "if you deny your faith of believing in heaven." (They would not even say "God.") None of the twenty-five gave in.

So they, too, were killed. The officials used a steamroller to crush them to death. It was a slow, excruciating death, in front of the whole village, which had been brought to watch. But before it was over, one of the Christians began to sing "More Love to Thee." The final verse of the hymn says:

> Then shall my latest breath
> Whisper Thy praise.
> This be the parting cry
> My heart shall raise;
> This still its prayer shall be:
> More love, O Christ, to thee.
> More love to Thee,
> More love to Thee!

A young lady who witnessed this terrible execution had been so traumatized by the images that she actually repressed the memory for a long time. Years later she went to a Gospel meeting, and they sang that song, "More Love to Thee." All of a sudden, the memory came back to her and she began to scream and cry. The people around her were scared, but they began to pray, and they calmed her down, and then she told her story. Later, we heard the story from three others to confirm it was true.

That's how the North Koreans tried to destroy Christianity. We once thought no believers were left in North Korea, but God is mightier than the Communist!

The Bible League Report

From Tragedy
To Triumph

She is a glimmer of light following some dark days. She is confidence in the wake of uncertainty. She is strength and hope and the youthful persona of unfailing faith. She is the face of triumph over tragedy.

She is Melissa (Missy) Jenkins. And she is now just a little famous. She's been interviewed by most of the national media. She's been on the cover of magazines, featured in several and even had her first prom documented by *People Magazine*.

Opportunity has presented itself to wheelchair bound Missy Jenkins because of the tragic turn in her life on December 1, 1997. On that well-remembered day in the Paducah community, 15-year-old Missy was hit by one of 14-year-old Michael Carneal's bullets, which left three girls dead and Missy unable to move her legs.

Now, more than two years later, Missy has triumphed over that disastrous day and proven to many, including herself, that great strength can come from a faith in God and a willingness to work hard. In that two years, Missy has capitalized on the opportunities which have come her way and scorned the limitations with an energy and determination that perhaps only God knew she had.

"Because of this experience, I'm a whole lot stronger than I ever knew I was. Maybe I've grown up. I always thought something like this would never happen to me, but it did. The most important lesson I've learned through all this is to never stop believing there is a God. Things like this are going to happen, but He will help us through them," the ever-positive Missy comments about her struggle to fight back from the debilitation of that fateful gunshot.

It's clear that Missy has allowed the gunshot-inflicted disruption in her life to slow her down only slightly. Local businesses and contractors donated the supplies and labor for a 1,600-foot-handicapped-equipped addition to the family's ranch-style home that allows Missy to zip around her new surroundings much more easily. "Mom doesn't call it our apartment," says Missy. "But that's what it's like."

A group of local automobile dealers gave her family a wheelchair-accessible van and after finally getting her license, Missy has now been able to learn to drive her own flashy black Mustang to the mall and all points asunder. She resumed her place in the marching band, she sung her heart out in the 2000 presentation of *Kaleidoscope*, Heath High School's end-of-year song and dance performance. She has been a girl on the go almost from the moment she was able to sit up and take charge of the situation following her initial hospitalization at Lourdes Hospital.

"I've done a lot more in my wheelchair than I ever thought about before the shooting," Missy says with a girlish giggle. Her most recent stay in California at the Walk Again Rehabilitation Center afforded her the opportunity to meet Jay Leno and enjoy his show. She also had a chance to visit the set and meet the cast of the NBC show Frazier. A visit to Disneyland was a similar highlight of her California stay.

Also during her rehabilitation period, Missy met and spoke with President Clinton about youth violence. She later spoke to fifth grade students in West Virginia's DARE program and this summer, was a panel participant on violence held in Orlando, Florida and sponsored by FCCLA.

Still there are moments of quiet when the cameras abate and the lights dim and Missy meets the reality from which she cannot escape—life in a wheelchair—at the hands of a child with a gun.

"She cries sometimes," admits Mandy, speaking out of her sister's earshot. "Like at school concerts. She'll just get frustrated about not being able to walk...I think she'll walk again. But if she doesn't, Missy knows she can live her life in a wheelchair if she has to."

Either way Mandy will be at her sister's side. "We were close to begin with," says Mandy, who acts the part of a personal physical therapist, lifting Missy out of her chair. "We've always had this best-friend relationship where it's more than being a sister and more than being a friend. I can't think when I've ever done anything big without her." Missy agrees: "She's been with me the whole time."

In fact, it was Mandy who protectively flung her body over that of her sister after Missy fell to the floor that frightening December morning. As the bullets started flying, one suddenly cut through the left shoulder of Missy's black Adidas shirt. "I think I was the second one shot," says Missy, who initially felt no pain. "Nicole was first. Mandy and I were standing together. I thought it was a joke at first, because it sounded like firecrackers." As she fell to the floor, Missy realized that she had been shot. "I knew from the start I was paralyzed," she says. "I couldn't feel my stomach. I told Mandy, and she said, 'Be strong! Don't die.'"

"She was the calm one," says Mandy, who miraculously escaped unharmed. "She helped me stay calm. I saw more than Missy. I saw Michael shooting and blood was everywhere. I felt a bullet go through my hair...Missy didn't see anything, but she got it worse than all of us."

Missy spent the next five months in hospitals recovering from her wounds. From intensive care at Lourdes in Paducah to the Cardinal Hill Rehabilitation Center in Lexington, Missy derived the strength to progress from lying flat for weeks on end to eight hours of daily physical therapy at Cardinal Hill.

"At first dressing myself took 45 minutes. Trying to learn how to do everything again, to be normal, was so hard it made me sick or wore me out. I also started learning how to get around in a wheelchair," Missy remembers. "They taught me how to do wheelies in the wheelchair, get over curbs and transfer myself to a bathtub or toilet.

At first it was frustrating, because there was so much I didn't know how to do and it was all very hard. But after a while it got easier and easier. It helped that they had former patients visit me and show me that I could still be able to go out and drive a car and that being paralyzed wasn't the end of my life. I also learned how to swim and bowl."

Of the five students who were hurt and survived that day, Missy suffered the gravest injuries and—given her wheelchair—the ones that remain the most visible. "Some times I feel like I'm always going to be a constant reminder of what happened," she says. "But then maybe there's a reason for that."

"At first I felt guilty that it should have happened to Missy," says Mandy. "But my mom said maybe Missy could handle more than most kids."

And so she has. By April of 1998, Missy had mastered maneuvering the light-weight, sporty wheelchair she now uses to get around—going everywhere from the bowling alley ("She's better now than she was before the shooting," says Mandy) to the mall, where the twins love to shop for makeup and have their nails done.

Incredibly, neither twin shows any anger toward Michael Carneal. Says Mandy, "As hard as it is, you have to forgive." Missy sums it up this way. "Holding an awful grudge in my heart doesn't bring back the girls who died. It doesn't help me get any better. But forgiveness gives you closure."

Closing the door on Missy's life-changing tragedy is one step forward to what lies in her future. With the help of her newly fitted walking brace, Missy walked across the stage at Heath High School in June to accept her diploma as a sympathetic nation looked on. Now that graduation is behind them, both girls are headed for their college experience at Murray State University. Missy will be rooming with her life-long friend, Kelly Hard. She plans to pursue a career in pediatric psychology, focusing on disabled youth.

But schoolwork and college life are but a part of Missy Jenkins' lifelong challenge. "Of course, I want to walk again, but when I pray, that's the last thing I pray for. I pray for everyone else who's coping with what's going on in the world, but especially I pray for my mom because she's in a wheelchair, too. She has arthritis.

I also pray for patience, because sometimes I'm not as patient as I wish I were. I plan to keep praying I'll get through this; I'll try my hardest and not give up. I saw people at the rehabilitation hospital who had given up. It just made their situation more difficult. They didn't get any better. I'll keep working hard and praying, I'll give it time and things will happen."

Missy feels strongly that things happen for a reason. She still questions why Michael Carneal chose to bring a gun to school on that winter day in 1997. But she's trying diligently to go beyond the past to focus on the future.

"A lot of people have told me my good attitude has been an inspiration to them. I think maybe that's my purpose," Missy concludes.

Darlene M. Mazzone

When Does God Pick Flowers

God reveals his purpose and mercy through the death of loved ones.

On October 26, 1981, I was involved in an auto accident that killed my wife, Phyllis, and my baby daughter, Elisabeth. My oldest daughter, Lisa and my two sons, Tom and Elsworth, were critically injured. At the hospital, the doctors told me that Lisa would never walk again and that after 72 hours they intended to pull the plug on the life support machines that were hooked up to Tom, my oldest son. God miraculously healed both Tom and Lisa! We came home from the hospital December fourth.

I would catch myself walking through the house as if

I were searching for something. I realized that I was looking for the two people who were no longer there. Since it was Christmas Eve, I was trying very hard to be happy with the three children I had left, but we were all so depressed. I went outside to pray, leaving the children in the house. I stopped and looked up into the heavens and I said, "Oh, God, WHY! Why didn't you take them on January twenty-sixth or February twenty-sixth? I'm not saying 'Why did you take them at all? I trust that what you did was right, but why couldn't you have just waited a couple of months? You know how much Phyllis loved to shop for Christmas presents. And you know how much Christmas means to a little 4-year-old girl—brightly colored Christmas trees, doll babies and secrets. If you would just have waited a few months!'"

It seemed that God shook his head, as if I'm slow to learn. He took His arm and He wiped away a whole section of the stars and I saw right into heaven. There was Phyllis with her back to me in a flowing, white robe. And there was Emil Matson, a converted alcoholic who had spent years at the Barberton Rescue Mission. He had memorized 1,000 chapters of scripture—he was there with Phyllis! I saw that the two of them were looking into a garden, a beautiful flower garden.

I saw that my little girl, Elisabeth, was crouched down, handpicking beautiful flowers from the garden and handing them to her Grampa, Phyllis's father, Ben Coy. She wasn't just grabbing any old flower; she was very carefully selecting each one. I knew how Elisabeth could pick flowers. Just the summer before, in our yard, I had held her hand as we walked and she picked "Dandy Lions." As she picked them one-by-one, she would hand each one to me and say, "Daddy, look at that Dandy Lion! It's just too pretty to pick!" I knew first hand how Elisabeth could pick flowers.

Watching her handing the flowers to her Grampa Ben, I saw the angels sort of pushing them on, trying to get them to hurry. I asked, "Oh, God, what is going on? What am I missing?" God then said to me, "Bruce, you don't know how to celebrate birthdays on earth. We know how to have birthday parties in heaven and it is Jesus' birthday party. That's why I took Phyllis and Elisabeth when I chose to. I wanted them to be here a couple of months before Christmas so they could be acclimated to the place. I didn't want them to feel like strangers their first Christmas in heaven (which is so special!) so I brought Elisabeth two months before Christmas and I didn't want her to come alone so I let her mother come with her. You see, Bruce, I didn't take them at the best time for you, I took them at the best time for them."

God doesn't snatch our loved ones from us as you would hurriedly snatch wild flowers from the roadside, but He carefully handpicks each one at the best time for them, not the best time for us.

Bruce Hawthorne

Columbine Killers Mocked Christ on Video

Eric Harris and Dylan Klebold blasphemed Christ and directed invectives at Christian students and others in a video prior to the killings at Columbine last year. The two made five videos before the shooting, venting their rage at athletes, minorities, and Christians, *Christianity Today* said.

"Go Romans. Thank God they crucified that [expletive]," Harris said making a vulgar reference to Jesus, CT said. Both teens then began chanting, "Go Romans" and cheering. "What would Jesus do?" Klebold yelled. "What would I do?" he said, pretending to fire a gun at the camera, the publication said.

The boys singled out Christian student Rachel Scott on the tape, calling her a "godly whore" and "stuck up," it continued. Harris mimicked her faith. "Yeah. 'I love Jesus. I love Jesus.' Shut the [expletive] up," he said. Scott had told Klebold and Harris about Christ during a class they shared, and confronted them about a violent video they made, her father, Darrell, said. She was one of the first to be killed in the attack.

The killers hated God, Darrell Scott said. "There seemed to be an extra element of hatred and vengeance there." Police allowed victims' parents to see the videos, which had not been released to the public, CT said. A *Time* magazine report included some details from the tapes but did not mention the anti-Christian elements.

A student sitting near Rachel Scott says God saved his life. Mark Taylor, 17, was shot twice from behind, and five more times in the chest as he sat on a hill outside the school talking about religion with his friends, the *Rocky Mountain News* said.

"I remember being in the ambulance, afraid of dying," he told Columbine Community Church January 26. "I called to God to save me and He answered my plea. I knew right then, I was certain God was going to save my life."

Doctors at University Hospital said they did not expect Taylor to live. "I'm looking at a dead man," a surgeon told Dr. Bill Deagle, who also spoke at the church. Taylor's mother said she couldn't understand why the shooting happened until she remembered a passage of Scripture about "all things coming together for the good," she told the *News*. "I said, 'Lord, all things?' And he said, 'All things.'"

religiontoday.crosswalk.com

Miracles Set Course For "God's Navy"

There's just no telling what will happen when God's people ask in faith for miracles and He takes them at their word. In the year 2000, for the first time in history, two decommissioned U.S. Coast Guard cutters—the *White Sage* and the *White Holly*—will set sail to provide much-needed medical missionary service in the North Pacific. The vessels are currently being refitted and reactivated following what was, literally, an "Act of Congress" last year.

Never before has a decommissioned Coast Guard cutter been released to a civilian organization to be placed into service; instead, these vessels are typically "recycled" as part of foreign aid packages or museums.

"We are able to obtain these vessels only because God took an active part in the proceedings," said Mike Hakanson, a chaplain in the U.S. Naval Reserve and a member of Canvasback Missions. "All the way through, we could see God's hand at work."

Canvasback is a nonprofit Christian medical organization providing health care to remote islands of the Pacific. For 14 years, Canvasback co-founders Jamie and Jaque Spence have operated a 71-foot catamaran, the *Canvasback*, which provides medical care and missionary outreach to the Marshall Islands and the Federated States of Micronesia.

46

These nations have long been plagued by poverty, poor health education, and a lack of modern health care—factors that have resulted in sometimes appalling conditions. Nearly half of the population—even some teenagers—has adult-onset diabetes; 63.3 babies per thousand will die in infancy; and half of the deaths of children under age five result from respiratory infections, malnutrition, pre-maturity and diarrhea. About one in three outer island children never grow up.

"Every year our mission grew and grew," said Jamie Spence. "By 1997, our medical ministry had outgrown the *Canvasback*. God directed me to start planning two new ships. I worked with a marine architect, and we designed the ships we would need to continue to meet the needs of the people our ministry had been created to serve."

Unaware of Canvasback's work, Hakanson had a similar dream of providing medical service in the South Pacific when he spotted a small vessel in a Fort Bragg, California, shipyard. The officer in charge recommended instead another vessel that might better meet his needs: the *White Stag*, a 133-foot Coast Guard cutter in the process of being demolished.

Hakanson learned that in order to get the *White Stag,* it would literally require an act of Congress. He was advised to find a representative willing to sponsor the bill. Congressman Frank Riggs, First District, California, agreed to support the measure.

"Then it hit me...I stood a good chance of acquiring a 133-foot ship—and I had no idea how to sail it!" says Hakanson. That's when he contacted Canvasback, discussed common goals and decided to join forces with the organization.

"When Mike contacted me, I was pessimistic at first, (but) I asked Mike to send me the plans for the *White Sage*. This ship was exactly what we needed, even down to the length and space layout. I knew God was leading," said Spence.

But Canvasback needed two ships, not just one. Spence called Hakanson back and said, "See if you can get your hands on another ship, too."

Though it seemed an impossible feat, Hakanson was amazed when he got a call from the Coast Guard, offering him another vessel, the *White Holly*, also a 133-foot cutter. The proposed bill was edited to read "two vessels" instead of one. "Then we prayed," Spence added. Their prayers were answered when the measure passed the House of Representatives.

There were still two more major hurdles: finding a senator to support the measure and identifying a larger, existing bill to attach it to, to ensure it reached the floor for a vote.

"And then, God took a hand again," Hakanson recalled. "Our friendly staffer in Congressman Riggs' office called us and said, 'I've got a bill for you. It's called the Coast Guard Re-authorization Act Bill. Your bill would fit perfectly as a rider.'"

The staffer directed Hakanson and Spence to the Senate Commission on Oceans and Fisheries. The name rang a bell; they had sent a fax to the commission four months before. "I called and was told, 'I'm so glad you contacted us! We got your fax, but couldn't read the contact line, so we didn't know who sent it,'" Hakanson remembered. "The office had wanted to reach us after the fax came to the attention of U.S. Senator Olympia Snowe, who determined it should be added to the bill. Her staff said this rarely, if ever happens. God had seen to it that our bill was protected."

The next morning, Hakanson awoke early and went into his office to do some work. On the desk was an unopened packet of information Jamie had sent on Canvasback. "I had never had a chance to read it, so I tore it open and began to go through it," says Hakanson.

"At 6 a.m. the phone rang. It was our contact at the Senate Commission on Oceans and Fisheries. They were in committee going through final revisions on the House and Senate versions of the bill, and wondered whether Canvasback could handle ships of that size. He began asking me questions."

Hakanson looked down at the sheet he was reading — the information being requested was literally in his hand. I read the answer. He asked another question. The answer was right there. We went through the packet, page by page, and it provided the answers to all their questions. If I hadn't had it in my hand right then, the bill probably would have been dropped.

The bill wasn't dropped. The bill was approved, the president signed it on November 13, 1998, and Canvasback had their ships! What's more, the bill was approved in such a way that Canvasback ended up with a "blank check" which allowed them to acquire a half million dollars worth of shore boats, tools and equipment off of their decommissioned ships to enhance the operability of the ships.

But there was a catch: The legislation included a clause requiring Canvasback to have $800,000 in a trust account for the operation of the vessels in order to take possession, and Canvasback didn't have the money. The organization was given about ten months—until September, 1999—to come up with the money and take legal possession of the ships. Despite fundraising efforts, Canvasback was unable to gather the dollars necessary.

"Mike and I went to the shipyard and got aboard the ships, still talking about whether or not we would be able to take possession of them in thirteen hours," Jamie says. While we were talking, Jamie got a message to call California. He called on his cell phone, talked a few minutes, then put his hand over the phone and said, "We have the $800,000!"

The money came from the Marshall Islands, where the Marshallese president and cabinet had just approved setting aside funds to be used in maintaining and supporting Canvasback's medical ministry to their islands. The funds were to be delivered in increments over the next four years—exactly what Canvasback needed in order to sign.

"We walked on the ship that morning as guests, and walked off that night as part of God's Navy," he says. "It was amazing!"

Canvasback has delivered about a million dollars per year in health care and medicine to the Marshall Islands. The Marshallese government, for an investment of about $800,000, has made it possible for them to not only continue doing so, but to double their services.

Both ships are in Baltimore for refitting, which is necessary for both documentation and insurance purposes as well as readiness to provide medical service.

"We have a shopping list," said Spence. "First, and most obviously, we need to raise funds to finish paying for the refit, the crew and the voyage to the Marshall Islands.

At that point, the trust account kicks in to pay for the upkeep and operation of the vessels."

"Equally important, we need volunteers, and qualified Christian seamen and women. There are lots of jobs for both skilled and unskilled volunteers to help get these ships ready for service."

"This is an exciting time, and a scary time," Spence added. "It has been incredible, seeing how God has held His hand over this whole process. We look forward to continuing our work with Him."

Norise Jastillana and Sandy Van

Canvasback Missions, Inc., 940 Adams St., Suite R, Benicia, Ca. 94510, can also be reached by phone (800-793-7245)

His Name Is John

His name is John. He has wild hair, wears a T-shirt with holes in it, jeans, and no shoes. This was literally his wardrobe for his entire four years of college. He is brilliant. Kind of esoteric and very, very bright. He became a Christian while attending college.

Across the street from the college campus is a well-dressed, very conservative church. They want to develop a ministry to the students, but are not sure how to go about it. One day, John decides to go there. He walks in with no shoes, jeans, his T-shirt, and wild hair. The service has already started, so John starts down the aisle looking for a seat in the already filled church. By now people are looking a bit uncomfortable, but no one says anything. As John gets closer to the pulpit, he realizes there are no seats, so he just sits down on the carpet. (Although perfectly acceptable behavior at a college fellowship, trust me, this had never happened in this church before!)

By now the congregation is really uptight, and the

tension in the air is thick. About this time, the minister realizes that from way at the back of the church, a deacon is slowly making his way toward John. Now the deacon is in his eighties, has silver-gray hair, is wearing a three-piece suit and a pocket watch. A godly man, very elegant, very dignified, very courtly. He walks with a cane and as he starts toward this boy, everyone is saying to themselves, "You can't blame him for what he's about to do. How can you expect a man of his age and background to understand some college kid on the floor?" It takes a long time for the man to reach the boy. The church is utterly silent except for the clicking of the man's cane. All eyes are focused on him. You can't even hear anyone breathing. People are thinking, "The minister can't even preach the sermon until the deacon does what he has to do."

Now they see this elderly man drop his cane on the floor. With great difficulty, he lowers himself and sits down next to John to worship with him so he won't be alone. Everyone chokes up with emotion. When the minister gains control, he says, "What I'm about to preach, you will never remember. What you have just seen, you will never forget."

Author Unknown

Where Healing Begins

I was expecting my daughter's call that morning, April 19, 1995. As I sat by the phone, my coffee cup rattled on the tabletop. The next instant, I heard a thunderous sound and...the floor shook beneath my feet. I ran to the kitchen window. Blue sky, spring sunshine. Just a peaceful Oklahoma day. It was hard to imagine anything terrible happening on a bright Wednesday like that.

I hadn't put on my Texaco uniform that morning; I was meeting my 23-year-old daughter, Julie, for lunch. Proud of her? Everyone who came in for an oil change heard what a great kid I had. She'd caught me bragging on her just two days before. "Dad! People don't want to hear all that!"

Odd, that visit...Julie often stopped by my service station for a few minutes on her way home from her job at the Murrah Building in downtown Oklahoma City (her mother and I were divorced). Monday, though, it was as if ...she didn't want to leave. She stayed two hours, then threw her arms around me. Julie always gave me a hug when she left, but Monday she held me a long time.

"Good-bye, Daddy," she'd said.

That was odd too. Nowadays Julie only called me Daddy when she had something really important to say. Well, maybe she'd tell me about it this afternoon. Every Wednesday I met Julie for lunch at the Athenian restaurant across from the Murrah Building.

At nine o'clock I'd sat down with a cup of coffee to wait for her call. Julie usually got to work at the Social

Security office where she was a translator at 8:00 a.m. sharp. It was her first job after college. As a federal employee, Julie got only 30 minutes for lunch—and she wouldn't take 31! She always called to find out what I wanted for lunch then phoned our order in to the Athenian so we could eat as soon as we arrived.

Chicken sandwich this time, I'd decided. The parking lot would be full by lunchtime; I'd see Julie's red Pontiac in her favorite spot beneath a huge old American elm tree. I'd park my truck at one of the meters on the street and watch for her to come out of the big glass doors—such a little person, just five feet tall ("Five feet one-half inch, Dad!"), 103 pounds.

But a big heart. I believed in loving your neighbor and all the rest I heard in church on Sundays. But Julie! She lived her faith all day, every day. Spent her free time helping the needy, taught Sunday School, volunteered for Habitat for Humanity—I kidded her she was trying to save the whole world single-handed.

The rumbling subsided. Bewildered, I stood staring out the kitchen window. Then the phone rang. I grabbed it.

"Julie?"

It was my brother, Frank, calling from his car on his way out to the family farm where we'd grown up. "Is your TV on, Bud? Radio says there's been an explosion downtown."

Downtown? Eight miles away? What kind of explosion could rock my table way out here! On the local news channel I saw an aerial view of downtown from the traffic helicopter. Through clouds of smoke and dust the camera zoomed in on a nine-story building with its entire front-half missing. An announcer's voice: "the Alfred P.

Murrah Federal Building…"

Floors thrusting straight out into space. Tangled wreckage in rooms with no outer wall. And in place of those big glass doors, a mountain of rubble three stories high. I didn't move. I scarcely breathed. My world stopped at that moment. They were appealing for people not to come into the downtown area, but nothing could have pulled me away from the telephone anyway. Julie would be calling. Her office was at the back of the building, the part still standing. Julie would find her way to a phone and dial my number.

All that day, all that night, all the next day and the next night, I sat by the phone, while relatives and friends fanned out to every hospital. Twice the phone rang with the news that Julie's name was on a survivor's list! Twice it rang again with a correction: The lists were not survivors, but simply of people who worked in the building.

Friday morning, two days after the explosion, I gave up my sleepless vigil and drove downtown. Because I had a family member still missing, police let me through the barricade. Cranes, search dogs and an army of rescue workers toiled among hills of rubble, one of them a mound of debris that had been the Athenian restaurant. Mangled automobiles, Julie's red Pontiac among them, surrounded a scorched and broken elm tree, its new spring leaves stripped away like so many bright lives.

Julie, where are you? Rescuers confirmed that everyone else working in that rear office had made it out alive. The woman at the desk next to Julie's had come away with only a cut on her arm. But, at exactly nine o'clock, Julie had left her desk and walked to the reception room up front, to escort her first two clients back to her office.

They found the three bodies Saturday morning in the

corridor, a few feet from safety.

From the moment I learned it was a bomb—a premeditated act of murder—that had killed Julie and 167 others, from babies in their cribs to old folks applying for their pensions, I survived on hate. When Timothy McVeigh and Terry Nichols were arrested, I seethed at the idea of a trial. Why should those monsters live another day?

Other memories blur together...Julie's college friends coming from all over the country to her funeral. Victims' families meeting. Laying flowers on my daughter's grave. No time frame for any of it. For me, time was stuck at 9:02 a.m., April 19, 1995.

One small event did stand out among the meaningless days. One night—two months after the bombing? Four?— I was watching a TV update on the investigation, fuming at the delays, when the screen showed a stocky, gray-haired man stooped over a flower bed. "Cameramen in Buffalo today," a reporter said, "caught a rare shot of Timothy McVeigh's father in his..."

I sprang at the set. I didn't want to see this man, didn't want to know anything about him. But before I could switch it off, the man looked up, straight at the camera. It was only a glimpse of his face, but in that instant I saw a depth of pain like—

Like mine.

Oh, dear God, I thought, *this man has lost a child too*.

That was all, a momentary flash of recognition. And yet that face, that pain, kept coming back to me as the months dragged on, my own pain unchanged, unending.

January 1996 arrived, a new year on the calendar, but not for me. I stood at the cyclone fence around the cleared site of the Murrah Building, as I had so often in the previous nine months. The fence held small remembrances: a teddy bear, a photograph, a flower.

My eyes traveled past the mementos to the shattered elm tree where Julie had always parked. The tree was bare on that January day, but in my mind I saw it as it had looked the summer after the bombing. Incredibly, impossibly, those stripped and broken branches had thrust out new leaves.

The thought that came to me then seemed to have nothing to do with new life. It was the sudden, certain knowledge that McVeigh's execution would not end my pain. The pain was there to stay. The only question was what I let it do to me.

Julie, you wouldn't know me now! Angry and bitter, hate cutting me off from Julie's way of love, from Julie herself. There in front of me, inside that cyclone fence, was what blind hate had brought about. The bombing on the anniversary of the Branch Davidian deaths in Waco, Texas, was supposed to avenge what McVeigh's obsessed mind believed was a government wrong...I knew something about obsession now, knew what brooding on a wrong can do to your heart.

I looked again at the tenacious old elm that had survived the worst that hate could do. And I knew that in a world where wrongs are committed every day, I could do one thing, make one individual decision, to stop the cycle.

Many people didn't understand when I quit publicly agitating for McVeigh's execution. A reporter, interviewing victims' families on the first anniversary of the bombing, heard about my change of heart and mentioned it in a story that went out on the wire services. I began to get invitations to speak to various groups. One invitation, in the fall of

1998, three years after the bombing, came from a nun in Buffalo...what had I heard about that place? Then I remembered. Tim McVeigh's father.

Reach out. To the father of Julie's killer? Maybe Julie could have, but not me. Not to this guy. That was asking too much.

Except Julie couldn't reach out now.

The nun sounded startled when I asked if there was some way I could meet Mr. McVeigh. But she called back to say she'd contacted his church: He would meet me at his home Saturday morning, September 5.

That is how I found myself ringing the doorbell of a small yellow frame house in upstate New York. It seemed a long wait before the door opened and the man whose face had haunted me for three years looked out.

"Mr. McVeigh?" I asked. "I'm Bud Welch."

"Let me get my shoes on," he said.

He disappeared, and I realized I was shaking. What was I doing here? What could we talk about? The man emerged with his shoes on and we stood there awkwardly.

"I hear you have a garden," I said finally. "I grew up on a farm."

We walked to the back of the house, where neat rows of tomatoes and corn showed a caring hand. For half an hour we talked weeds and mulch—we were Bud and Bill now—then he took me inside and we sat at the kitchen table, drinking ginger ale. Family photos covered a wall. He pointed out pictures of his older daughter, her husband, his baby granddaughter. He saw me staring at a photo of a good-looking boy in suit jacket and tie. "Tim's high school graduation," he said simply.

"Gosh," I exclaimed, "what a handsome kid!"

The words were out before I could stop them. Any more than Bill could stop the tears that filled his eyes.

His younger daughter, Jennifer, 24 years old, came in, hair damp from the shower. Julie never got to be 24, but I knew right away the two would have hit it off. Jennifer had just started teaching at an elementary school, her first job too. Some of the parents, she said, had threatened to take their kids out when they saw her last name.

Bill talked about his job on the night shift at a General Motors plant. Just my age, he'd been there 36 years. We were two blue-collar joes, trying to do right by our kids. I stayed nearly two hours, and when I got up to leave Jennifer hugged me like Julie always had. We held each other tight, both of us crying. I don't know about Jennifer, but I was thinking that I'd gone to church all my life and had never felt as close to God as I did at that moment.

"We're in this together," I told Jennifer and her dad, "for the rest of our lives. We can't change the past, but we have a choice about the future."

Bill and I kept in touch by telephone, two guys doing our best. What that best will be, neither of us knows, but that broken elm tree gives me a hint. They were going to bulldoze it when they cleared away the debris, but I spearheaded a drive to save the tree, and now it will be part of a memorial to the bomb victims. It may still die, damaged as it is. But we've harvested enough seeds and shoots from it that new life can one day take its place. Like the seed of caring Julie left behind, one person reaching out to another. It's a seed that can be planted wherever a cycle of hate leaves an open wound in God's world.

Bud Welch

Shooting Hero's Recovery "Miraculous"

To his doctor's amazement, John Montgomery has pushed himself up to a standing position with little help. He's even taken a couple of small steps.

Montgomery has done nothing but amaze people around him since late March, when he was shot five times in his upper body and head after giving himself up to an enraged shooter in a Galesburg business office.

No one knows how many lives Montgomery saved that day with the simple words, "I'm over here." Already wounded and down, he was then shot three more times. But his action prevented the gunman from harming other people hiding in the room.

Neurosurgeon Dzung Dinh, one of the first to treat Montgomery in the emergency room, said the prognosis was bad when the 45-year-old Tolono man arrived. Montgomery was semicomatose, on life support and had a deep bullet wound to the left side of his brain.

"We really didn't know how much recovery there would be," Dinh said. "But he's a fighter, very strong willpower, and that's very important."

During his three-month hospital stay, Montgomery was surrounded by his wife and three daughters, other relatives and friends. Former co-worker Steve Apsey said he came about a dozen times to visit and pray with Montgomery.

"Each time he looked better; he was moving, talking, talking better," Apsey said. "It was just miraculous—all those bullets going into him and not hitting anything vital."

Montgomery attributes his recovery to his physical strength, faith and strong family support. His wife, Vicki, said stubbornness has a little something to do with it, too.

"There were various times in our marriage that I didn't appreciate his stubborn streak," she said. "Now I'm very thankful for it."

Jessica L. Aberle

A Mother's Story

It's sorta weird how people use the word heartache with such intense feeling. Almost every time I turn on the radio, I hear a tune about somebody's heartache over a misbehaving lover. Or, I overhear folks at the next table at a restaurant chatting about how their child's frowning, downturned face broke their hearts because of this or that. Or, what about when people say it just broke my heart to pay that much money for such and such.

That's not a heartache.

Heartache is when you've spent a year fighting to save your child's life and doctors tell you they spot something irregular in her bloodstream just two months after her bone marrow transplant, when she is feeling great.

It's too soon for relapse, doctors say. Steroids typically cause this, they say, but we will do a bone marrow aspiration to check.

And that day, after all her fighting, and all her pain, we really, really learn about heartache.

That day, my husband's head dropped. In all my 18 years of knowing him, I had never, ever seen this before. He's a former football player. He always holds his head up and meets any situation head on.

But not that day. What he felt was pure heartache.

I watched him holding his head in his hands, rubbing his temples, almost trying to push the thought from his brain. He looked up at the doctor and nurses and then over at our daughter and shook his head.

Although bad news was not our friend, it also was not a stranger. Two days later our suspicions were confirmed. Our doctor was shocked.

Despite more than a year of turmoil and hardship, we had learned to take the good and make it better. We learned to grasp hope and hold on—tight. We worked hard not to linger too long on the negatives. We instead held out for a miracle.

It's amazing what we ask for and what we receive.

Let me explain.

PREPARING FOR THE WORST

I still remember the day Jade, our first-born twin, was admitted to Vanderbilt Children's Hospital. That was several months before her diagnosis. All we knew then was that she had a fever of 105 and something was wrong. At that time, any talk of leukemia was presented as one of several possibilities, but there were, at that time, no definite answers.

We had one thought—that if the absolute worst happened, and Jade had leukemia or some other diagnosis requiring a bone marrow transplant, she had a perfect match right beside her. I recall my brother-in-law telling me perhaps Jillian—who was showing no signs of illness—was sent to save her sister. I fell in line with that train of thought.

Since the day I was told I was carrying twins, I questioned how and why this fate was bestowed upon me. Multiple births did not run in our family. We didn't even know I was carrying twins until late in the pregnancy. So in our family, we thought of them not only as surprises but also as miracles.

Anyway—we held onto that thought of some type of miraculous transfusion or transplant that would essentially make all of this go away.

So, to find out which members of our family might be a match for Jade in case she needed a bone marrow transplant, we went in to have our blood tested.

We found out that I wasn't a match, and Irvin wasn't a match, and our son Myles was not a match.

But that wasn't the worst news we got that day.

The blood revealed that Jillian had the same cancer as her sister.

There was no way they could help each other.

Our twin daughters, Jade and Jillian, one year olds, were diagnosed with acute myelogenous leukemia (AML) in 1999—Jade in February and Jillian in July. This form of leukemia, more often seen in older adults, had taken hold of our precious girls.

IN SEARCH OF A MIRACLE

For nearly a year, my husband Irvin and I have asked for two miracles. Actually, it's not just the two of us;

hundreds of people have been praying for the same miracle.

It was quite simple, we thought—heal and cure our girls; a request, not uncommon when dealing with life-threatening illnesses.

So we all prayed for a dual miracle. All the while we prayed and rocked, sang and laughed, cried and worried, we asked for the healing of our girls. That their tiny, innocent bodies be renewed and filled with healthy cells. We asked that the cancerous cells that had invaded their bodies disappear.

As the year progressed, both girls were hospitalized for six-month treatment regimes. As Jade was completing her chemotherapy treatments, Jillian was beginning hers.

Finally, we thought our miracle was coming to fruition.

But we were slighted. Jade relapsed within weeks of coming home. We were given two options—forgo treatment or continue with more chemotherapy in hopes of prompting a second remission in preparation for a bone marrow transplant.

Wow. We honestly didn't think it would come to that.

Sure, we were told that the chemotherapy treatments could kill her. We were warned about all the potential infections that could invade her body, eventually taking her. We were counseled on the many side effects that intensive chemotherapy treatments could cause to a child's body, including potentially severe problems with the heart, liver and lungs.

Despite having to shoulder the burden of such wrenching decision, we continued our prayer vigils.

Our hearts ached from the questions and decisions that swirled in our brains. Irvin and I felt there was only one choice that was right for Jade. We had to try. We had to give her a chance. The miracle could still happen.

But who would save our child? Her sister, her five-year-old brother, her father and I could not help her. We felt helpless. Was there anyone listening to our faithful request for miracles?

200 MILES AWAY

A marrow donor was found and Jade got a second chance at life.

She went through a series of chemotherapy and radiation treatments, received her transplant in Cincinnati November 20. Because of the donor gift we were able to celebrate the girls' birthday on December 1 in Cincinnati.

For six weeks, Jade and Irvin were 200 miles away. We all chatted on the phone, sent e-mails and shared funny stories daily about our lives. During that time, Jade definitely became a daddy's girl in every way. She even wore her Titan's football bandanna with pride on game days.

And all the time Jade was undergoing her treatments, we had another sick child to take care of here. Jillian paid her dues at Children's Hospital—which we affectionately called Camp Vanderbilt—and was home recuperating. She had done remarkably well. Unlike her sister, there were no return visits to the hospital for infections or other adverse reactions to therapy. Not that her experience with chemotherapy was an easy one, but it was far less full of surprises than her sister's.

Jade and Irvin came home from Cincinnati on December 23. What a perfect Christmas gift! We were all home for Christmas and were able to welcome the millennium together. Not to mention being able to enjoy the simple, quiet, everyday pleasures of being with Jade, like her infectious laughter or her determination, her big brown eyes or her soft chubby body as she lay curled in our arms.

Unfortunately, Jade relapsed again in January. But this time, there was nothing anyone could do. We lived and loved almost in desperation for four weeks, and she kept her ever-resilient attitude until she earned her angel wings on February 4th.

We were blessed by literally hundreds of people who baby-sat for us, brought dinners, helped with a community-wide yard sale/fund raiser, who participated in a bone marrow drive to try to find a donor for Jade, and, most important, in a thousand small ways, let us know they cared and that we were loved.

All along we had been praying, asking, and begging for a miracle to save our twins.

It's amazing how you get what you ask for. We asked that Jade and Jillian be healed, cured, be without pain and cancer. That they both be happy, fulfilled and examples of life to all who encountered them.

It's not easy to accept, but we got our miracle.

THE MIRACLE OF PEACE

Jade saved her sister's life — at least that's how we see it. Without Jade's warning, Jillian's cancer might not have been caught in time. We believe that she was sent to forewarn the doctors that her sister was carrying cells that would develop, some day, into cancer. That choice was made, long before I ever felt them kick or held them.

Jade is no longer in pain; she is at peace and she is healed. It's just not in the way we thought it would happen. It's not the way we wanted it to be.

Jillian continues to be in remission and doing superbly. We must all remember that the miracle of life continues on—it just doesn't always happen the way we plan it.

Although the heartache my husband felt on that day back in January will never be forgotten, and I am not sure completely healed, it will be softened by the wonderful gift Jade left him—her unconditional love.

In the quiet moments after Jade's passing, my husband tiptoed back into the room and thanked her for letting him love her so much and for her loving him without any barriers or stipulations. It's a bond they will always share.

Jade will forever be a miracle to us. We continue to be amazed at her strength, her zest for life and overall ability to share her love with all who came in contact with her.

And for Jillian, Jade is the angel sent to watch over her, always. And that is the kind of comfort that only a miracle can bring.

Jessica Pasley

A Child's Mite

Mark 12:42-43 "But a poor widow came and put in two very small copper coins, worth only a fraction of a penny. Calling his disciples to him, Jesus said, "I tell you the truth, this poor widow has put more into the treasury than all the others."

A sobbing little girl stood near a small church from which she had been turned away because it 'was too crowded'. "I can't go to Sunday School," she sobbed to the pastor as he walked by. Seeing her shabby, unkempt appearance, the pastor guessed the reason and, taking her by the hand, took her inside and found a place for her in the Sunday School class. The child was so touched that she went to bed that night thinking of the children who have no place to worship Jesus.

Some two years later, this child lay dead in one of the

poor tenement buildings. The parents called for the kind-hearted pastor, who had befriended their daughter, to handle the final arrangements. As her poor little body was being moved, a worn and crumpled purse was found. It seemed to have been rummaged from some trash dump. Inside was found 57 cents and a note scribbled in childish handwriting which read, "This is to help build the little church bigger so more children can go to Sunday School." For two years she had saved for this offering of love.

When the pastor tearfully read that note, he knew instantly what he would do. Carrying this note and the cracked, red pocketbook to the pulpit, he told the story of her unselfish love and devotion. He challenged his deacons to get busy and raise enough money for the large building.

But the story doesn't end there! A newspaper learned of the story and published it. It was read by a realtor who offered them a parcel of land worth many thousands. When told the church could not pay so much, he offered it for 57 cents.

Church members made large subscriptions.

Checks came from far and wide. Within five years the little girl's gift had increased to $250,000 – a huge sum for that time (near the turn of the century). Her unselfish love had paid large dividends.

When you are in the city of Philadelphia, look up Temple Baptist Church, with a seating capacity of 3,300; and Temple University, where hundreds of students are trained. Have a look, too, at the Good Samaritan Hospital and at a Sunday School building which houses hundreds of Sunday scholars, so that no child in the area will ever need to be left outside during Sunday School time. In one of the rooms of this building may be seen the picture of the sweet face of the little girl whose 57 cents, so sacrificially saved, made such remarkable history. Alongside of it is a portrait of her kind pastor, Dr. Russell H. Conwell, author of the book, "Acres of Diamonds."

This goes to show WHAT GOD CAN DO WITH 57 CENTS!!!

Author Unknown

What Money Can't Buy

Jorge Valdes became the U. S. head of Colombia's powerful Medellin drug cartel, thanks to his intelligence, drive and unshakable will. In this position, he had presidents of countries bow to him, women flock to him, and every "pleasure" millions could buy. But, in the end, it wasn't prison, the government or his colleagues in crime that forced him out. It was his 2-year-old daughter, Krystle, who unwittingly led him to a second chance at life.

The first-born son of Cuban immigrants, Jorge worked long hours to help them start over in Miami. His parents raised him to value independence, honesty and family. Then an acquaintance introduced him to drug trafficking. It quickly gave him everything this world had to offer. It also led to beatings, torture and five years of imprisonment in Panama. Jorge's endurance of these trials increased his benefactor's trust in him.

"I had Lear jets, Rolls Royces, a fleet of cars and

bodyguards." Jorge recalled in an interview with *Family Voice*. "You do something that is satisfying for the moment, but then you need a greater dosage. You think, 'One woman doesn't satisfy me, maybe two, three or four will.' I tried everything the world has to offer."

A LITTLE CHILD LED HIM

After eleven years, this indulgent life left Jorge empty, totally devoid of hope or purpose. Even money no longer enticed him. He repeatedly violated his marriage, and his wife Sherry left, taking Krystle and her younger sister, Jade, with her. Jorge remained with Jorgito, his young son from a previous marriage. He wallowed deeper in pornography and perversion.

Then, Sherry unexpectedly dropped off Krystle for an overnight visit at his home, where Jorge was entertaining two women. After he tucked Krystle into bed, they resumed their partying and eventually fell asleep—until Krystle came tapping on his door, calling for her daddy.

Horrified at the thought of his little daughter discovering him, Jorge forced the women to leave through a window.

"I wanted to check on Krystle, but I was too dirty, I wanted to run to her, to hug her tightly, but I felt so filthy," Jorge writes in his book, *Coming Clean* (Waterbrook Press). "I stumbled toward the shower, turned on the water as hot as I could stand, and tried washing away my foulness."

This incident finally made Jorge face the decadence of his life. It caused him to leave it all—the power, prestige, money. He told his Colombian business partner he was walking away. Convinced of his loyalty, they let him go.

WASHED CLEAN

During his years in the business, Jorge had never snitched on anyone, had never ordered a beating or killing. He had been at the top. No one had reason to kill him. Still, for a few weeks he lived in fear. Gradually, it went away, and Jorge lived on his Florida ranch and developed his horse breeding business. He studied karate with Tim Brooks, but Tim had something much more important to pass on to him: Jesus Christ.

Before the divorce became final, Sherry and Jorge had a baby son, Alex. To help deal with the pain of separation from his children, Jorge focused on learning karate. Tim, his wife Teruko, and their friends presented the Gospel to Jorge through words and action. Their peace and contentment—even without an abundance of material possession—intrigued him. At first, he suspected they were putting on an act.

But finally, Jorge's misery overpowered him. Though surrounded by wealth and about to be remarried, he came face to face with the pain his life had produced for his children, his parents and brother, for countless lives destroyed by the cocaine he had trafficked. He knelt to pray.

"Jesus, I don't know if what Tim has been telling me is true or not," Jorge prayed. "But Jesus, there is something about these Christian people that I want. If you will help me change and give me this peace and tranquility (that they have), I'll give You my whole heart. As much as I have lived for the devil in the past, I will do ten times as much for You."

Jorge said, "My sense of tranquility was deep and

unfathomable. I felt clean! I felt clean on the inside—as though all the dirt of my life had suddenly been power-washed away."

TOTAL TURNAROUND

His life began to change in subtle ways. He became convicted of his use of profanity, of his intimate relationship with his fiancée, Margaret. He stopped using pornography, although the desire for it remained several years. He came to recognize Jesus as his close Friend and the sacrifice that bought his salvation. God was preparing Jorge to face perhaps the greatest challenge of his life.

"Whatever my eyes desired I did not keep from them. I did not withhold my heart from any pleasure...Then I looked on all the works that my hands had done... and indeed all was vanity...For God gives wisdom and knowledge and joy to a man, who is good in His sight." Ecclesiastes 2:10-11, 26

In 1990, Margaret and Jorge married. While they traveled on their honeymoon, a U.S. marshal arrested him. Though he had left the drug business several years earlier, Jorge found himself facing fifteen life sentences without the possibility of parole, charged with conspiracy to import narcotics.

"I didn't ask God to deliver me from this trial; I knew I was guilty, and I knew I had to somehow pay for my crimes," Jorge said, "and I truly wanted to do so, because I wanted to come clean."

The case against him greatly weakened when a key witness died in a plane crash. Still, Jorge refused to plead innocent. The prosecutors made an offer: all his money, property, horses—everything—as a trade-off for the possibility of serving reduced prison time. Jorge pleaded guilty as charged. Almost overnight he went from having millions to having nothing. Sadly, his marriage to Margaret did not survive.

The desire to come clean could have cost Jorge his life in prison. At the sentencing hearing, federal agents—who had helped build the case against him—testified that Jorge's faith in Christ had genuinely changed him.

Miraculously, the judge gave Jorge only ten years. He entered prison in Georgia, where he began taking courses through a Bible college. In 1993, he earned his bachelor's degree, and he continued to study, entering a master's degree program by correspondence.

STARTING OVER

One of the hardest aspects of imprisonment was the toll on Jorge's relationship with his children. Jorgito went to live with his mother in Miami. Sherry and her children moved, leaving no way for him to contact them. Finally, a year after his arrest, God opened a door for Jorge to locate them. He stayed as involved with his children as he could, doing homework over the telephone each day with Jorgito. He experienced the joy of leading 5-year-old Jade to Christ over the telephone. In time, all of his children came to Christ.

The miracles continued. After Jorge had served more than four years, the judge reduced his sentence to five years! On March 5, 1995, he was released on parole from federal prison. "All totaled, I had served close to ten years—one fourth of my life—in prison," he said.

Upon his release, Jorge set out to rebuild his relationship with his children. He became entirely open with them. "I took all the blame for the divorces," he said. "I told them what a horrible human being I was outside of Christ. I was open to them, and that was difficult."

Jorge later earned his doctorate in New Testament studies and obtained his dream job: teaching at a major university in Chicago. He married Sujey, a wonderful Christian. But the death of his beloved father caused Jorge to long for a closer relationship with his children, who now lived in Atlanta.

"Will they remember (me as the one) who sent a monthly check? The one they spent summers with?" Jorge asked. His answer: That wasn't enough. At the same time, he felt God leading him away from teaching and into a new calling.

"I did a gang revival in Chicago, and I saw 10-year-old kids come forward crying like I'd never seen anyone cry before. That day, I felt His voice saying He had not saved me to be a college professor," Jorge said. "I felt this is where I belong."

Jorge founded Coming Clean Ministries, a youth evangelism organization, and moved to Atlanta, where he lives within three miles of his children. Last year, he and Sujey became parents to Estevan, whom his siblings joyfully welcomed.

Through his ministry, Jorge has developed keen insight into the typical inner-city gang member. His father is in jail or totally uninvolved, so the gang leader becomes a "father" to him. He provides the structure to chaotic lives. "(The gang member) has come into this world without hope," Jorge said. "His only (hope) is to make it through today, then through tomorrow. He's not even thinking of a few days from now."

"To these kids, my message is that they don't have to give up and live as if there were no tomorrow. God cares about them and (gives them) a new beginning."

Coming Clean Ministries works beyond the inner city with another group of needy young people: upper middle-class kids in suburbia. "'We've done everything right.' That's what mothers say when they bring their children to me," Jorge says. "But you will never see an inner-city child pull a gun on someone and then shoot himself. White suburban kids want to pull a gun on 100 others. Then they want to kill themselves."

"It is good for me that I have been afflicted, that I may learn your statues. The law of your mouth is better to me than thousands of shekels of gold and silver." Psalms 119:71-72

RESCUE FROM DEATH

He tells of meeting a clean-cut 14-year-old who grew up in the church, and yet fell into drugs. "I said, 'You know what I'm about to tell you isn't from someone who had heard about it. I lived it,'" Jorge recalled. "'The road you're on is going to lead you to imprisonment, for a long time, or to death. Pray that you won't be killed, because in jail you have a chance to turn your life around.'"

The young man looked at Jorge with a deadly stare. "Sir...I want to die," he said.

"I've been around hired killers who don't have the evil I've seen in these kids," Jorge said. "(They're) like walking time bombs."

Jorge points to failing families as the major cause of crime and despair. In the cities, most families are poor and fatherless. In the suburbs, some kids are raised "right" but choose to stray. Many other times, "Parents have substituted presence with possessions. But (young people) want their mom and dad," Jorge says. "One study found that the average parent spends six minutes a day one-on-one with his or her child."

"In my family, we eat together and deal with issues together. We pray, do devotions, read and watch TV together. That doesn't happen much anymore, because (people) want a big house and big cars. I used to made $2 million a month, but I am happier now, barely surviving."

Jorge has plans for reaching today's youth. He aims to fill stadiums with kids, to change their hearts and minds through the power of Christ, to provide a network for follow-up and programs to help free people from pornography and drugs.

"I can't do a lot about the past, but I can do a lot about the future," Jorge says. "I want to empower these kids to be Generation X. In Greek, 'X' means 'of the cross'. I want to refocus them into changing their world for Christ."

Pamela Pearson Wong

The Carpenter's Glasses

Mother's father worked as a carpenter. On this particular day, he was building some crates for the clothes his church was sending to some orphanage in China.

On his way home, he reached into his shirt pocket to find his glasses, but they were gone. When he mentally replayed his earlier actions, he realized what happened; the glasses had slipped out of his pocket unnoticed and fallen into one of the crates, which he had nailed shut. His brand new glasses were heading for China!

The Great Depression was at its height and Grandpa had six children. He had spent $20 for those glasses that very morning. He was upset by the thought of having to buy another pair. "It's not fair," he told God as he drove home in frustration. "I've been very faithful in giving my time and money to your work, and now this."

Several months later, the director of the orphanage was on furlough in the United States. He wanted to visit all the churches that supported him in China; so he came to speak one Sunday at my Grandfather's small church in Chicago.

The missionary began by thanking the people for their faithfulness in supporting the orphanage. "But most of all," he said, "I must thank you for the glasses you sent last year. You see, the Communist had just swept through the orphanage, destroying everything, including my glasses. I was desperate. Even if I had the money, there was simply no way of replacing those glasses. Along with not being able to see well, I experienced headaches every day, so my coworkers and I were much in prayer about this. Then your crates arrived. When my staff removed the covers, they found a pair of glasses lying on the top."

The missionary paused long enough to let his words sink in. Then, still gripped with the wonder of it all, he continued: "Folks, when I tried on the glasses, it was as though they had been custom-made just for me! I want to thank you for being a part of that."

The people listened, happy for the miraculous glasses. But the missionary surely must have confused their church with another, they thought. There were no glasses on their list of items to be sent overseas.

But sitting quietly in the back, with tears streaming down his face, an ordinary carpenter realized the Master Carpenter had used him in an extraordinary way.

Author Unknown

PASTOR DONATES KIDNEY

A pastor says he wasn't trying to be a hero, but just obeying God. Gale Janofski, pastor of Brookhaven Wesleyan Church in Marion, Indiana, was sitting next to pastor Rick Jett at a ministerial association dinner a few years ago. Jett, an acquaintance, mentioned he was on a waiting list to receive a kidney transplant, according to *The Wesleyan Advocate,* a denominational magazine.

"It was as if the Lord actually came up behind me, put His hands on me physically, and impressed me with this thought, 'Maybe you could help him, Gale,'" Janofski said.

After a lot of prayer, discussions with his wife, and examination of his motives to make sure he wasn't "just trying to impress people with my offer to help," Janofski offered Jett his kidney, he said.

"It just kind of blew me away," Jett said of their meeting. "I had been discouraged and I was seeking encouragement from God. Then two days later Gale walked into my office."

Jett had undergone kidney dialysis for two years, three days a week, each treatment taking 5 1/2 hours, according to *The Advocate.*

….After a battery of tests, examinations, and X-rays, the men were found to be a *perfect match* for a transplant. The surgery was performed in February, 1999, and both men are doing well.

"I am overwhelmed by God's leading in each and every step of this whole process," Janofski said. He said he is grateful to the Wesleyan denomination and his local church for their support during his recovery period after the operation before he could resume his ministerial duties.

religiontoday.crosswalk.com

Miracle in the Mountains

For mankind it is often difficult to see the hand of God in tragic situations. Sometimes, however, an incident occurs that is so amazing and miraculous that it is impossible not to see God's presence in the midst of the storm. This is the story of such an incident, a story of a young man, his family, and the night God showed a community that miracles still happen.

Speedwell, Tennessee, is a community that lies approximately 10 miles from the Cumberland Gap region where Daniel Boone blazed his famous trail. Nestled amidst the beauty of forested ridges, lush farmlands, and cool lakes, Speedwell is the type of small town where yard sales are plenteous in warm weather and dogs still ride in the back of pick-up trucks. Family is important in Speedwell, as is religion. Not the new-fangled religion displayed on television, mind you, but the old-time religion of Sunday dinner-on-the-ground and baptism in the river. It is safe to say that Speedwell is a good place to raise a family and grow up learning the traditions and customs of life as it was meant to be before food could be bought at a drive-through window and "download" became something you did with a computer instead of a piece of farm equipment.

At the age of 15, Eric Overton has lived his entire life in Speedwell. He is one of those kids who went to church nine months before he was ever born and has been raised in a close, loving family. Eric and his younger brother Ryan are exceptional athletes who love sports and the outdoors. Eric is the vice-president of the local FFA chapter. Eric and Ryan, along with their parents, Darryl and Angie, are active members of Haynes Flat Baptist Church, where Eric is the song leader. Eric's involvement in his church, the choir, and the youth group is not typical of many teens today. The term "good kid" is used often to describe him. Perhaps it is this extraordinary fact and his faith that took him through the horrible events that unfolded one night in his young life...

Saturday, October 28, 2000, was a day of celebration and happiness on the Overton Dairy Farm. Members of the church and community gathered to enjoy the 20th Annual Haunted Hayride that promised good times and good food. The evening was to end with the traditional hayride around the farm and through the "haunted" woods. People loaded the wagon for the ride, but Eric and his best friend, Adam Powers, chose to ride behind the wagon on an ATV, what people around Speedwell call a 4-wheeler. Eric and Adam would drift back from the wagon then come charging up in the dusk, without the headlight on, to scare the unsuspecting people on the wagon. It was completely dark when the wagon of tired revelers headed for home. Eric, driving the 4-wheeler, and Adam, hanging on behind him raced ahead of the wagon for a final scare. In the darkness, Eric went over the cattle crossing, down a slopped field, and into a barbed wire fence. Eric was nearly decapitated on impact as the barbed wire became entangled around his throat. In the darkness, Adam began searching for his friend. It was then that the first miracle of the evening occurred. Out of the blackness, a light shone on Eric, helping Adam to find him and see the extensive wound. Adam describes the light to be "like a spotlight." Eric was lying on his back with his feet up over the fencing. Adam picked Eric up and set him on the 4-wheeler, still entangled in the barbed wire.

In the confusion, people on the hayride began to realize that something was wrong. Eric's dad Darryl and William Jessie, Eric's football coach, were the first to arrive at the accident. What they found when they approached the gully will forever be etched in their minds. Eric was bleeding profusely from a gash that, literally, almost extended ear to ear. Jessie recalls having the feeling of "stark terror." "My first impulse was to run," says Jessie. But the "courage inspired by Jesus Christ" allowed him to stay and help in the attempts to save Eric's life. Frantically, Darryl, William, and Adam tried to free Eric from the sharp barbs of the fence. The wire was wrapped around the 4-wheeler, Eric, and the ankles of the men. Then, like the miracle of the light in the darkness, the fencing just "fell off," and they were miraculously able to free Eric and themselves from the wire. They placed Eric in the back seat of a pick-up truck and raced for the hospital in LaFollette, Tennessee, twenty miles away. In the truck, Darryl and Angie prayed all the way to the hospital.

It was no accident or coincidence that Coach William Jessie was in attendance at the festival that night. A former military policeman and deputy, Coach Jessie was skilled in EMT procedures, CPR, and other life-saving techniques. It is also no accident that Coach Jessie found himself in the back seat of the pick-up that night on the ride to the hospital, cradling Eric's head in his arms with a coat wrapped around the wound. Because of his experience with these types of situations, Coach Jessie knew exactly how to hold Eric's head so as to prevent his bleeding to death while still allowing airflow. Once at the hospital, the ER doctors assessed Eric's condition and immediately had him airlifted to the University of Tennessee Medical Center in Knoxville. Back home, as news of the horrible accident began to circulate, prayers were being said for the life of Eric Overton.

The wait in the lounge at the UT Medical Center was agonizing for Eric's parents, family members, and friends. Was it possible for someone to survive injuries of Eric's extent? If Eric survived, would there be brain damage? Paralysis? Would he be able to speak again? It was apparent that Eric, once again, would need a miracle. As doctors worked to repair Eric's torn throat, over 100 people filled the ER waiting area to comfort Eric's parents and to pray for that miracle.

The miracle came. The cut to Eric's throat was so deep that his larynx and esophagus were severed, but no main arteries, amazingly, were damaged. When Eric's mother asked the doctor how this could be, he replied that his only explanation was that it was "the hand of God." One outcome, however, was the fact that Eric had lost his voice, a devastating blow yet so small when compared to the life of an extraordinary young man.

Miracles, it seems, have become a way of life for Eric Overton, for the boy who lost his voice one night in a terrible accident still talks and sings in church. Fitted with an artificial voice box (TEP), Eric is able to speak and live a normal life with a few adjustments. But life is about adjustments and change and courage to face those changes. Most of all, however, life is about miracles, and for a small community in the shadow of the Cumberland Mountains, a miracle breathes and sings and lives among them.

Kelli Little

Just in Time

My prayer partner, Art, and I meet often to share and pray for each other, our families and for those needing salvation.

Pete Peterson is one of the most outstanding examples of our prayers for someone's salvation.

Pete's wife had come to our church for some ten years, but her husband was cold as stone to the Christian message. Art and I decided to make it a matter of intense prayer concern.

Then all of a sudden Pete sold his house and moved to California, where he purchased a gasoline service station.

It was discouraging at first, but we kept praying for another three months. Then I received a speaking invitation for a retreat in California and, checking the map, discovered the campgrounds were only seven miles from Pete's town!

"I'll keep praying while you're there," Art promised.

First chance I had, I got in touch with Pete. He was

surprisingly open and friendly. I found it easy to talk to him.

"Pete," I said as we got down to the point, "you've run as far as you can from God. Today is the day for you to make a decision to receive Christ as your Savior."

Pete looked squarely at me, his eyes glistening.

"You're right," he said.

We knelt there in his home, as Peter Peterson became a new creature in Christ. That night he came to the retreat where I was speaking and gave a wonderful witness. His wife told us later how rapidly he grew in the Christian life.

Art and I spent a good while thanking God for the answer to our prayers.

But the greatest impetus for gratitude came three weeks after my return when I received a telephone call from Mrs. Peterson.

"Pete's dead," she sobbed. "There was a holdup at his service station, and the bandit shot him through the head. Oh, I'm so thankful you helped him to come to Christ before he died! He was so happy in his new Christian faith!"

Dr. Stanley Tam

The Miracle of the Tablecloth

The brand new pastor and his wife, newly assigned to their first ministry to reopen a church in urban Brooklyn, arrived in early October excited about their opportunities. When they saw their church, it was very run down and needed much work. They set a goal to have everything done in time to have their first service on Christmas Eve.

They worked hard, repairing pews, plastering walls, painting, etc. and on December eighteenth were ahead of schedule and just about finished. On December nineteenth a terrible tempest—a driving rainstorm hit the area and lasted for two days. On the twenty-first, the pastor went over to the church.

His heart sunk when he saw that the roof had leaked, causing a large area of plaster about six feet by eight feet to fall off the front wall of the sanctuary just behind the pulpit, beginning about head high.

The pastor cleaned up the mess on the floor, and not knowing what else to do but postpone the Christmas Eve service, headed home.

On the way he noticed that a local business was having a flea market type sale for charity so he stopped in. One of the items was a beautiful, handmade, ivory colored, crochet table cloth with exquisite work, fine colors and a cross embroidered right in the center. It was just the right size to cover up the hole in the front wall. He bought it and headed back to the church. By this time it had started to snow. An older woman running from the opposite direction was trying to catch a bus.

She missed it.

The pastor invited her to wait in the warm church for the next bus forty-five minutes later. She sat in a pew and paid no attention to the pastor while he got a ladder, hangers, etc., to put up the tablecloth as a wall tapestry. The pastor could hardly believe how beautiful it looked and it covered up the entire problem area.

Then he noticed the woman walking down the center aisle. Her face was as white as a sheet. "Pastor," she asked, "Where did you get that tablecloth?"

The pastor explained. The woman asked him to check the lower right hand corner to see if the initials EBG were crocheted into it there.

They were.

These were the initials of the woman, and she had made this tablecloth thirty-five years before in Austria.

The woman could hardly believe it as the pastor told her how he had just gotten the tablecloth. The woman explained that before the war she and her husband were well-to-do people in Austria. When the Nazis came, she was forced to leave. Her husband was going to follow her the next week. She was captured, sent to prison and never saw her husband or her home again.

The pastor wanted to give her the tablecloth, but she made the pastor keep it for the church. The pastor insisted on driving her home; that was the least he could do. She lived on the other side of Staten Island and was only in Brooklyn for the day for a housecleaning job.

What a wonderful service they had on Christmas Eve. The church was almost full. The music and the spirit were great. At the end of the service, the pastor and his wife greeted everyone at the door and many said that they would return. One older man, whom the pastor recognized from the neighborhood, continued to sit in one of the pews and stare, and the pastor wondered why he wasn't leaving. The man asked him where he got the tablecloth on the front wall because it was identical to one that his wife had made years ago when they lived in Austria before the war and how could there be two tablecloths so much alike?

He told the pastor how the Nazis came, how he forced his wife to flee for her safety, and he was supposed to follow her, but he was arrested and put in a concentration camp. He never saw his wife or his home again for all the thirty-five years in between.

The pastor asked him if he would allow him to take him for a little ride.

They drove to Staten Island and to the same house where the pastor had taken the woman three days earlier. He helped the man climb the three flights of stairs to the woman's apartment, knocked on the door and he saw the

greatest Christmas reunion he could ever imagine.
Everything happens for a reason....

A True Story – Submitted by Pastor Rob Reid
Vanguard Magazine

God Brings Revival to Public School

What started as a special presentation by the Pearl River Central High School's Fellowship of Christian Athletes turned into a full-fledged revival that has transformed the school in Carriere, Mississippi, and left school administrators astounded.

Nearly 90 percent of the school's 670 students attended the program, which was originally scheduled for one hour. But when the bell rang, there were more than 100 students standing in line to pray and make spiritual decisions.

"It was heart-stopping," said Pearl River principal Lolita Lee. "When I realized how many students needed to pray, I went ahead and let the program continue." And continue it did for more than four hours. Through three class periods and lunch, students wept, prayed, sang, and made amends with one another.

Following a hastily arranged telephone call to the school superintendent, Lee went back to the gymnasium where the revival was taking place. "Who was I to say to these students, 'Hey, you aren't important. Go back to class.'"

And a month later, Lee said the results of the revival are manifested in the school. "I've had teachers and staff tell me how much better the students are," she said. "Our hallways are filled with students who say how their lives have been changed."

The spiritual awakening all started a month earlier when a group of FCA leaders met with their faculty sponsor to discuss plans for the remainder of the school year.

"Everyone was writing down goals and plans when suddenly a teacher suggested we reach our school for Christ," said Cary-Anne Dell, a member of FCAs' leadership team. "That's pretty much how it all got started and the Lord took it from there."

The plan involved an in-school rally during which FCA members would perform skits and share testimonies about what it means to be a Christian. A team of 16 students wrote skits and prepared the rally—all except for the closing. "We just decided that the Lord was going to figure out the closing," Dell said.

Dell said the FCA members shared their plans with churches throughout the area. "We had people praying for us all over south Mississippi," Dell said. "It was incredible to see how all those prayers were answered."

One prayer involved a sound system. The acoustics in the school's gymnasium were terrible, Dell said, "We didn't have a sound system so we started praying. The next day, two churches called the school and offered to provide one."

Since the entire event was student-led and student-organized, Lee said the club didn't have to seek permission from the school board.

At first, she said she was skeptical of the meeting. "You know how it is with kids wanting to get out of class," she said. Midway through the skits, however, the principal felt it was obvious the Spirit of the Lord was moving. "I even had tears in my eyes," said the veteran educator.

"You should have seen God working," Dell said. "It

was so awesome. I had the chance to lead someone to the Lord right there in the gym."

At one point, Lee said she counted 120 students lined up to share testimonies and be counseled. "And keep in mind," Lee added, "this was entirely student-led. Our staff only observed."

For Dell, who will spend a good portion of her summer as a missionary to Haiti with Teen Mania Ministries, the experience was unforgettable. "It is so wonderful to be chosen by God to do His work," she said.

As for Lee, she said she hasn't suffered any repercussions by allowing the revival to span the course of a school day. "So far, so good," she said. And even if there are, Lee said looking back, she would do the same thing again. Lee may be reached at *llee@prchs.k12.ms.us*.

Todd Starnes

Jian Found Jesus and Went to Prison For His Faith

Cheng Jian was poor, but he was not unhappy. He had to work very hard every day to provide for himself, his wife and their five children in their tiny riverside village in northern China.

More often than not, they couldn't really make ends meet, and they sometimes did go hungry. But Jian was optimistic, and everyone in the village liked to have him around because of his easy laughter and good attitude.

The darkest shadow on Jian's horizon was his wife's frail health. For years she had been too sick to do any steady work, so Jian had to work doubly hard in the fields. When she could work, Jian's wife was ill tempered because she was suffering so badly.

Jian struggled on, until one day he witnessed something that changed his life.

In a nearby village, he saw a huge commotion, and when he drew near, discovered the Chinese authorities forcing an elderly woman to parade through the village to be pelted with stones and abused by the crowds.

She was a Christian being punished for her faith.

Yet to Jian's amazement, this old woman did not hang her head or stumble in shame as the crowds pressed in on her. Instead, she boldly proclaimed her faith in Jesus: "My family was very poor and we were always ill. Even I had seven different kinds of sickness. I spent a lot of money on medicine and I have suffered a lot. But since I came to the Lord, we have had peace in my family."

Jian understood nothing about Jesus at all, but he did hear the woman say that her whole family had been sick, and now they were well!

He hurried home to his own village and spoke to every single person he knew who professed to be a Christian. He asked them to come and pray for his wife.

What a wonderful life it would be if only she could be made whole, he thought.

The Christians of Jian's village were frightened of him. They thought the authorities might have sent him as a spy! But eventually they believed that he sincerely wanted prayer, and they came to his home.

For three successive days, groups of local Christians prayed for Jian's wife. And God completely healed her!

The very next day, the other workers in the field could hardly believe it when Jian's wife joined them… and then they were further amazed that she did not complain and lash out at the others, but worked hard—and smiled!

"What happened to you?" they asked. The only other people they knew who were so serene were the other Christians. They demanded of Jian's wife: "Have you believed in Jesus?"

But she had no answer for them, for neither she nor Jian had made a commitment to Christ. She knew that Jesus had healed her, but she had not become a Christian. And as for Jian, he said because she was the one who had received God's touch, it was up to her to choose Jesus or not—he wanted nothing to do with it.

Then a few nights later, Jian heard his wife crying in their home as she gave her heart to Jesus…and he, too, felt the power of God all around him. Both of them joyfully became Christians that night!

Not long after that, Jian was called to be a preacher.

Remember, the villagers had always loved having Jian around because of his cheerful attitude and easy laughter. Now that he knew Jesus, Jian's heart was truly joyful, and he was a wonderful witness of the Gospel.

He began to travel the countryside, encouraging the believers and leading others to Jesus.

So many poor and despairing people first began to believe the Word and receive the salvation of Jesus because of Jian's ministry. His example gave them the courage to take heart and have faith!

But there were people who were not happy about Jian's new-found calling. The Chinese authorities heard Jian was traveling the region, sharing the good news of Jesus—and they wanted to stop him!

Late one winter night when Jian returned home from a ministry-training seminar, he felt a stirring in his spirit that something was not right. He went into his backyard to be alone, and in spite of the bitter cold and vicious winds, he knelt in the ice and snow and began to pray.

Jian poured out his heart to God, asking for mercy for himself, his family, his people and his nation. Hours passed as he prayed, and tears streamed down his face as he knelt motionless in the snow.

Finally, another small stirring in his heart, and Jian heard the voice of the Holy Spirit: "Within three days, you will be arrested for the sake of the Lord."

Now Jian had peace. He knew what was to happen, and he trusted God to provide for him and his future, no matter what. He went into his house and fell asleep, knowing that his life was in God's hands.

It was three nights later that Jian and several other Christians were arrested as they left a meeting of a house church. Although they did not resist arrest, the authorities beat them mercilessly anyway.

Through a miracle of God's grace, Jian felt no pain as he was viciously beaten with clubs. This enraged his captors, for they wanted to see him cry out in pain. They beat him all the harder, until he finally passed out.

This was the beginning of seven months imprisonment for Jian.

He was tortured day after day, starved, beaten, humiliated.

But the other prisoners soon noticed something different about Jian. No matter how badly beaten he was, no matter how horribly he had been treated, he still seemed joyful in his spirit.

He was always ready to comfort another prisoner, always able to smile in spite of his pain.

The others were amazed by his attitude, and they even

asked him to sing for them. He did, and he also shared the Gospel with them.

One morning, Jian awakened singing, "Today is a beautiful day/ It's the day that the Lord has made/He causes me to feast in the presence of my enemies/The Lord is with me today." Minutes later, a van came and took him away.

The other prisoners were impressed. They thought that Jian had been singing that it was a beautiful day, and then he had been freed from jail. They began to discuss the Gospel he had shared with them, and several of them gave their lives to Christ.

Sadly, Jian had not really been set free when the van came and took him away. Rather, he had been taken to another interrogation.

When Jian refused to deny Jesus, the communist authorities whipped him, and even branded his fiesh with a hot iron.

For months the torture continued...until one night as Jian prayed in prison, the voice of the Holy Spirit spoke to him again: "When the trees begin to bud, you will leave this place."

Jian's heart filled with joy, for spring was not far off.

And not long after, he arose one morning to find the tiny bud of a twig from the tree just outside his window.

"Lord, I praise you," Jian cried. "Although I don't know what lies ahead, I commit everything into your hands. Keep me, Lord," he prayed.

And the Lord did just that.

China Fire

"I'll Go to Work in Your Place"

As I drove to the hospital, I prayed about how to offer to help my friend. Charles had been in a car accident, and now he lay in the intensive-care unit with multiple broken bones and severe internal injuries.

Having recently retired after 44 years of pastoring churches, I considered myself an expert at making hospital calls. Even as I prayed, I began planning how I could help Charles, a man 25 years my junior.

By the time I reached the hospital, I had decided what I would do. I would become God's handyman—mow the grass, run errands for Charles's wife and drive their two children to elementary school. I thought that I could also manage to contribute a modest check to help with their family expenses. Charles worked in the seafood section of a local supermarket and was the breadwinner for his family of four. It was obvious that he wouldn't be behind the seafood counter for a while.

Now, looking back on the events that followed, I wonder if God had been trying to impress on me the truth of Isaiah 55:8: "'My thoughts are not your thoughts, Nor are your ways My ways,' says the Lord."[1] For while I had prayed for guidance on how to help Charles, I had quickly made plans that seemed sensible to me without waiting to see how God might want to direct me.

---

[1] Isaiah 55:8, NKJV.

As I stood at Charles' bedside, my heart went out to him. He looked through pain-glazed eyes at me. A cap of bandages covered the top of his head, and his mangled left foot was elevated above the bed and hanging from the metal framework of the bed.

To my dismay, I soon became aware that my carefully developed plans to help Charles had totally missed the mark.

"Tom, I'm in trouble," he said. "They're not going to hold my job."

"Of course they will," I replied. "They wouldn't..."

"Oh, they'd manage for a while," he interrupted. "But the doctors can't predict how long the surgeries and the rehabilitation will take. The market will have to hire and train someone else."

My response astonished *me* almost as much as it did Charles. I heard myself saying, "I'll go to work in your place until you get on your feet again."

"You will?" he asked as relief flooded his face.

I left the hospital incredulous at what I had offered to do. I had no retail experience, and my knowledge of seafood was limited to an occasional meal at the local restaurant.

To my amazement, my offer was well-received by the manager of the supermarket. I was told that they would be glad to have me if I could clear it with the union. I thought that the interview with the union would put a stop to this plan, but they too were cooperative. I signed the necessary papers and later made arrangements to turn over my paycheck to Charles.

As I drove home, I struggled to come to terms with what was happening, God had called me to be a minister of the Gospel, a "fisher of men."[2] Was he now actually calling me to a second career? To selling fish at the local supermarket? I wanted to be obedient to the Lord Jesus, and I reasoned that He must have opened the doors leading to this unfamiliar work that I had agreed to perform. And hadn't I preached about people in the Bible who were called to unknown destinations? Abraham, for example: "By faith Abraham obeyed when he was called to go out....And he went out, not knowing where he was going."[3]

The Holy Spirit must have impressed on me the worthiness of Abraham as a role model because gradually I sensed peace about the new venture. In fact, excitement overtook my feeling of inadequacy as I set off for my first day of work at the supermarket.

Soon I was deep into on-the-job training. I found that I actually enjoyed my work. I especially liked serving customers. Repeat customers became friends. When I wasn't just filling orders, I studied reference books about seafood preparation and serving so that I could talk knowledgeably about "my products."

I like to think that what the Apostle Paul wrote to the Colossians permeated my performance: "Whatever you do, work at it with all your heart, as working for the Lord."[4] I wanted my behavior to be a witness to my faith. I wanted my life to demonstrate Jesus' words: "Let your light so shine before men, that they may see your good works and glorify your Father in heaven."[5]

---

[2] Cf. Matthew 4:19

[3] Hebrews 11:8,NKJV

[4] Colossians 3:23, NIV

[5] Matthew 5:16, NKJV

I worked for more than two months before Charles was finally permitted to return to work part time. The woman who managed the seafood department asked me to stay and work alongside Charles until they could determine whether he could handle the hours of standing on his injured foot. It soon became apparent that he could not, but Charles was elated when the store's personnel manager offered him a desk job in the computer area.

Then the manager of the seafood department came to talk to me, saying, "Tom, you know you can't leave us now." I agreed to stay on while they searched for a permanent replacement. After they found someone, she prevailed upon me to stay on at least part time.

Eventually my primary calling as a minister of the Gospel of Jesus Christ began affecting my "second career" in interesting ways. I have been involved in behind-the-scenes counseling with various store employees. I conducted a wedding service for a young woman in the meat department and a graveside service for the infant son of a man who worked elsewhere in the store.

Now I marvel at the multiple blessings that stemmed from the unexpected answer to my prayer about how to help my friend. I am enormously grateful that God enabled me to assist a family in an unexpected way. And I am even more thankful for the invaluable lesson concerning the importance of obedience to God, even if the directive seems farfetched.

I have learned that God will always help me to fulfill whatever He calls me to do. I need not be anxious when God calls me to do something different because "with God all things are possible."[6]

---

[6] Matthew 19:26, NKJV

By Tom Ballard as told to Gwen Lam
Decision Magazine

Search Ends Happily

A Kiwanis club in our state invited me to speak at their luncheon on the topic of how God became my senior partner.

The editor of the local newspaper attended and was so impressed by what God had done for me that he ran excerpts of my testimony as a church page feature. As a result, I received a letter from an attorney in New Castle, Pennsylvania, a former resident of the town where I had spoken.

"Send me details on the legal procedure you went through to make God your senior partner," he wrote. "I'm interested in this as an attorney."

I sent him the information, also including the plan of salvation.

Upon reading my letter, he telephoned.

"I've got to see you at once," he said. "Could I come to your office tomorrow afternoon?"

"Of course," I told him. "I'll be looking for you."

It was a drive of over two hundred miles.

"You may be just the person I've been looking for," he began, moments after entering my office. "I need spiritual help."

"I'll assist you any way I can." I assured him.

"I attended law school at the University of Michigan," he continued. "When I graduated, ready for my career, I thought I would have a sense of satisfaction, but I didn't. It was quite the contrary. I knew I needed spiritual guidance, so I sought out a clergyman in Ann Arbor and told him my problem. He was very kind. I have no doubt that he tried to be helpful. But the best he seemed able to do was recite a few platitudes. I didn't find the peace I wanted in my heart."

"Then I moved to Canton, Ohio, where I had taken a position in a law office. I was busy learning the ropes, but my spiritual need hung over me like a sword on a thread. So I looked for a church in Canton. Here, again, the pastor was very kind. In fact, he was a wonderful fellow. I attended the church regularly. But nothing seemed to add up."

"I had a chance to better myself by moving to New Castle. First thing I looked for was a church. By this time I was feeling rather desperate. You know, in the law business you see people on their most sordid side, and this surely didn't help any."

"Well, it was a repeat performance at the third church. Then I read your story in our hometown newspaper that I take just to keep in touch, and I said to myself, this is what's wrong with me. I don't give enough money to church. I figured if I'd do the way this fellow in Lima does, I might at least begin to find some meaning in life. That's why I wrote to you. But frankly, you confused me with that Bible verse from Ephesians. How does it go?"

"For by grace are you saved through faith: and that not of yourselves; it is the gift of God: not of works, lest any man should boast," I quoted.

"Could you explain that to me?"

That afternoon this Pennsylvania attorney knelt in my office and received the grace of God through faith in Jesus Christ. Peace came at last to his heart. We've kept in touch, and it's thrilling to learn of the many ways God is now using him as a Christian attorney to bring peace to others.

Dr. Stanley Tam

The Power of Prayer

A missionary on furlough told this true story while visiting his home church in Michigan…While serving at a small field hospital in Africa, every two weeks I traveled by bicycle through the jungle to a nearby city for supplies. This was a journey of two days and required camping overnight at the halfway point.

On one of these journeys, I arrived in the city where I planned to begin my two-day journey back to the field hospital. Upon arrival in the city, I observed two men fighting, one of whom had been seriously injured. I treated him for his injuries and at the same time talked to him about the Lord Jesus Christ. I then traveled two days, camping overnight, and arrived home without incident.

Two weeks later I repeated my journey. Upon arriving in the city, I was approached by the young man I had treated. He told me that he had known I carried money and medicines.

He said, "Some friends and I followed you into the jungle, knowing you would camp overnight. We planned to kill you and take your money and drugs. But just as we were about to jump your camp, we saw that you were surrounded by twenty-six armed guards."

At this I laughed and said that I was certainly all alone out in that jungle campsite.

The young man pressed the point, however, and said, "No, sir, I was not the only person to see the guards. My five friends also saw them, and we all counted them. It was because of those guards that we were afraid and left you alone."

At this point in the sermon, one of the men in the congregation jumped to his feet and asked if he could tell him the exact day that this happened.

The missionary told the congregation the date, and the man who interrupted told him this story: "On the night of your incident in Africa, it was morning here and I was preparing to play golf. I was about to putt when I felt the urge to pray for you. In fact, the urging of the Lord was so strong, I called men in this church to meet with me here in the sanctuary to pray for you. Would all of those men who met with me on that day stand up?"

The men who had met together to pray that day stood up. The missionary wasn't concerned with *who* they were–*he was too busy counting how many men he saw. There were twenty-six!!*

Author Unknown

God Honored Martyr's Death

Nearly 700 years ago, in 1315 AD according to Christian researcher, George Otis, a lone Spanish missionary had come to what is today Algeria, in northern Africa. He was the first missionary to Algerian Muslims, ancestors of the Kabyle people. His message of "Christ crucified and risen" met with great resistance. It is recorded that, while he was proclaiming the gospel in the marketplace of a small town, he was stoned. Some accounts say he died on the spot. Others record that he died later on board a ship. After rejecting the gospel, many generations of Kabyles lived and died without knowing about Christ. Then God honored the death of this martyr.

Near the very spot where his blood was spilled, two Kabyle men were having morning coffee in a café. One was visibly disturbed. For the night before, he had a vivid dream, like a vision. He told his friend about a Man in white who stood before him saying, **"I am Jesus. I am the way, the truth and the life. If you want to know God, you must know Me."**

As he shared his story, the jaw of his friend dropped and his eyes grew wide. Stunned, he was certain that his friend thought him crazy. I suppose he might have feared he could have reacted against him violently.

Instead, his astonished friend leaned over the table and said, "I had exactly the same dream last night!" Others in the café had been listening. One by one, each reported they had had the same dream! Eventually, it was learned that <u>every man, woman and child in that little town had seen the risen Christ in a dream</u>!

During the next six months, the people of this town sought out the gospel and four hundred people gave their lives to Jesus and were baptized. From this little town alone there resulted an 18-fold increase in the number of Christians in the entire nation!

What I find so fascinating is that, after almost 700 years of silence, this "divine initiative" happened just two years before the Kabyle translation of the "JESUS" film was completed!

Paul Eshleman
"The Jesus Film Project Newsletter"

God Answers Prayer

It was a typical Sunday. This day started like all the others. My husband Tim, my daughter Heather, and I got up, got ready and went to Sunday School and church. The services were good as usual. We came home, ate lunch and started planning what we were going to do this afternoon. We love the outdoors and we love to ride 4-wheelers. Riding 4-wheelers was the way we spent many Sunday afternoons. Another couple always rode with us. Sometimes there would be anywhere from three to fifteen people riding with us.

For some reason, this Sunday, I decided I wasn't going to go. It had turned cool and I didn't like to get cold. Heather didn't like to ride as much as I did; so she didn't want to go today either. I decided to stay home with her. I told her we would snuggle on the couch and take a nap. So Tim left to go riding with about six other people and Heather and I took a nap.

All of a sudden, I woke from a deep sleep and a strange feeling came over me. It wasn't really fear, it just felt like God was telling me to pray for Tim. I knew that some of the guys he was riding with weren't the safest riders in the world. When you get a bunch of them together like that, sometimes they like to clown around and that scares me. I am a safe rider and I want to keep *all* my body parts in tact. I began to worry that they were clowning around and somebody had gotten hurt. All I knew to do was what God told me to do – so I prayed.

Heather woke and asked me what I was doing. I told her I was praying for Dad and the others. She asked if they were okay. I told her yes that I just felt like God wanted me to pray and for her to go back to sleep. Everything was okay. She went back to sleep. I went and sat in the rocking chair and continued to pray.

About thirty minutes had passed when the phone rang. It was Tim. My heart sank. It was good to hear his voice, but I felt like something was wrong. He said, "Hey, Vic."

I said, "What's wrong?"

He continued, "I'm okay, but I think I've lost the 4-wheeler." (This was my brand new yellow 450-4-wheeler– my most favorite one I've ever had!) I told him I didn't care as long as he was okay! He continued to tell me what happened.

They were riding in a place they had ridden at least a thousand times before. It had rained a lot and the water had been over the roads. That was typical for this certain place, water always got out there. Tim and Jonathan were riding in front. Gary had to stop and help Cody with his 4-wheeler, so Tim decided to turn around, stop and wait for them.

When he pulled to the edge of the creek bank to turn around, the whole levy gave way!! Tim and the 4-wheeler went upside down into the creek! The place where he fell in was about fifteen feet deep. Since it had rained so much, the current was very swift and it was very cold. He was wearing coveralls, gloves, boots and a sock-to-boggin. His clothes were so heavy and the current was so fast that he almost drowned!

He was trying to hang onto the 4-wheeler, trying to stay afloat himself and trying to grab onto branches to keep from going down the river. The place where he fell was a fork in the creek that was only a short distance from entering the river. He said he knew if he couldn't stop before he got to the river, he would drown. Jonathan started trying to throw him a chain. The chain wound around the back tire and caught on to the 4-wheeler, but the current was so swift that it sank to the bottom. Tim said he either had to save the 4-wheeler or save himself; so he let go of the 4-wheeler and tried to grab branches of the trees to hang on to.

Right before you enter the river, there was a tree that had fallen over on the bank. He grabbed on to the trunk and hung on until he could pull himself up. He got up on the other side of the bank and took off his gloves and coveralls so he wouldn't be so weighted down when he went back across. He lost his sock-to-boggin somewhere in the struggle. He threw his coveralls across the creek. They threw him a rope and pulled him back across.

He couldn't find the 4-wheeler. He was too tired to jump back in and look for it. One of the other guys went in and tried to find it. He found it, but they couldn't pull it up. They tried to pull it out with a truck but the current was too swift. They called Bro. Ronnie to come and help. Gary went to get his tractor and boom to try and lift it out.

This was when Tim decided to call home. He said he was fine, just freezing.

Gary was able to lift the 4-wheeler out of the water. They checked the 4-wheeler. *It didn't even have any water in the oil and it didn't have a scratch on it!* The handlebar had caught on the root of a tree. This kept it from going into the main channel of the river. It cranked right up and he rode it into the back of a truck and came home

After he told me all that happened and after he calmed down, that's when I told him what had happened at home and how God was watching over him.

I asked him "About what time did this happen?"

He told me it happened at almost the exact time I said I was praying. He went on to add that he knew God was watching over him. When he was getting ready to go, he went to put on his hip boots, but they had a hole in them, so he put on a short, light weight pair instead. If he had had the hip boots on, they would have immediately filled with water and he said he didn't think he could have made it out alive.

So many times when we think things are just coincidence, it's really just God in control. I know God is always in control of everything, but I also know God hears and answers prayer! I shudder to think what might have happened that day if I hadn't prayed.

Vickie Bailey

Broken Bodies, But No Broken Spirits in Prison

Mother Lin is a brave Chinese evangelist, and she is well-known to China's believers and to the prison officials-for she has spent plenty of time imprisoned for her faith.

Yet this dear saint never stops proclaiming the love of Jesus, even when she has been unfairly arrested and treated terribly by the communist authorities.

It was during one of her many stays in prison that Mother Lin—along with several other imprisoned believers—received particularly horrendous punishments.

They discovered that another prisoner, who was serving 20 years, had agreed to spy on them and report their activities in return for receiving a lighter sentence.

The believers were locked into horrible solitary confinement cells for weeks on end, and Mother Lin received daily, ferocious beatings.

The Chinese Christians bore their persecution bravely, but the thing, which seemed worst about the situation was that they had managed to bring a few Bibles into prison with them—and those who did not have Bibles had worked diligently to hand-write the Scriptures for themselves.

Now that they had fallen under the wrath of the guards, those Bibles were sure to be discovered and confiscated! How could they survive without the precious Scriptures to comfort them?

But the Holy Spirit had impressed their hearts to hide their Bibles and little scraps of Scripture as best they could, and somehow these were never found by the guards!

Knowing that the guards would be looking for their Bibles (because the spy had reported them) they did leave some handwritten Scriptures out for the guards to find— they left evangelistic Gospel verses like John 3:16, Mark 1:15, Roman 3 and so on.

These verses explained the plan of salvation, and if the guards read them, they would learn how to accept Jesus as Savior!

The guards found the tracts, and they severely punished those who had written them. Two of the ladies were locked in a freezing pitch-black cell, which was partially flooded with frigid, filthy water.

One of these women, Yah Shen, received eight horrible beatings. The prison warden interrogated her, shouting, "Speak! Who led you to believe in Jesus? Where did the Bibles come from?"

But Yah Shen followed the example of our Savior as

He faced Pontius Pilate, and she did not open her mouth to speak a word.

"How dare a little criminal come before me eight times and not utter a word? Today, if you don't speak, I will beat you to death!" cried the warden.

Yah Shen said nothing and silently prayed for God's help.

The warden became so infuriated with her that he threatened her with an electric cattle prod!

Yah Shen had suffered so much already...her body was bruised and bloody. Yet this man had no mercy. If she would not cooperate, he would use the cattle prod on her.

To stun cattle, this horrible weapon is set for relatively low voltage, but for Yah Shen, he turned the power up to HIGH. There was every possibility that she would be killed when he attacked her with it—-

But at that moment, the Holy Spirit enveloped Yah Shen in a protective little cocoon, and when the warden ordered a guard to stun her with the cattle prod, nothing happened!

It was charged to full power, and the guard was holding it fast against her skin, yet she felt no pain, and there were no sparks, no seizures, nothing!

Now the warden was enraged!

He thought the cattle prod was malfunctioning, and he turned it on a nearby guard dog—which howled in anguished pain, began to froth at the mouth, and then flopped over completely unconscious!

The cattle prod was working, but it would not work on Yah Shen. They tried once again to torture her, and once again the Lord preserved her. When the other guards saw this miracle, they were filled with terror. Finally they understood the power of the God whose children they had been persecuting.

They rushed Yah Shen back to her cell...all the way, she sang hymns of praise to God for saving her from her persecutors.

Not long after this, another young woman was singled out for torture—because she had been one of those who copied Scriptures and songs for the other believers.

She had beautiful handwriting and worked very quickly. Her lovely scraps of Scripture and Gospel lyrics gave such comfort to the other Christians in chains...but when the authorities discovered what she had been doing, they placed her in handcuffs and made her wear them constantly.

Not only could she not write, but also she could barely feed herself.

And climbing into her top bunk each evening was a nightly torture, for she could not hold onto the bed, but was forced to pull up by the manacles fastened over her bleeding and swollen hands.

The handcuffs cut into her flesh mercilessly, and she lived in constant pain.

The non-believers who knew why she was being punished taunted her: "You always say your Lord is true and alive and is an omnipotent God—Have Him loose your handcuffs then!"

Although she suffered terrible, she did not lose heart. And finally one night she prayed:

"Lord, it is only right that I should be bound and handcuffed for Your sake and I am willing to do so. Yet, so that your Name will not be reproached any longer, and that many more may believe on You, I ask You to loose these handcuffs."

"Lord, as you caused the chains to fall off Peter, so cause these chains to fall off me! For You are not only Peter's God and Paul's God, You are also my God..."

At the end of her prayer, the handcuffs released themselves and fell to the ground!

In the morning, the guards were astounded!

"What did you use to open these handcuffs?" they demanded.

She replied, "They opened of themselves, and I don't know how they did so."

The guards knew that there was no way she could have loosed herself from the handcuffs, for they had the only key. They did not think the other inmates could have helped her, even if they had not been afraid to do so—

Suddenly, the guards were stricken by fear!

This woman worshiped the same God as the woman who was unaffected by the cattle prod torture. What an awesome God He must be!

As the news of the two miracles circulated through the prison, both inmates and guards alike were convicted by the power of God's Holy Spirit—and many came to the Lord!

Mother Lin reported, "This women's prison became a totally new place. The majority of the prisoners repented and believed in the Lord!

Although the believers were tortured, their bodies broken by the brutality of the evil communist authorities, their spirits were never broken—and God's Spirit reigned!"

China Fire

Martyr's Widow Carries On

A year after her husband and sons were murdered, Gladys Staines continues to serve in India. Graham, Philip, and Timothy Staines died January 23, 1999, when a mob stirred up by Hindu radicals set fire to the car in which they were sleeping near the village of Manoharpur in Orissa State, news reports said. The deaths touched off protests against nationalist Hindu groups and started a nationwide debate on religious conversions, *The Week*, an Indian news magazine, said.

Staines, 49, forgave her husband's killers and assumed his duties at the Mayurbhanj Leprosy Home, 100 miles from Manoharpur. She oversees the facility, where about 60 patients receive medical treatment and vocational training, she said. Patients who are rejected by their families even after they are cured live at the ministry's "rehabilitation farm," where they work at dairy and vegetable farming; their children receive free education at a local school.

"I was a housewife, virtually not involved in Graham's work. Now that he's gone I've taken on all the responsibility," she said. She visits the home several times a week to check on patients' progress and take care of the facility. She is working to fulfill her husband's dream of building a 40-bed hospital on nearby land.

Gladys met Graham in 1981 on a mission trip to India.

They married two years later and spent the next 16 years raising their family and ministering to people in Orissa State. Their three children were born in India and considered the country their home, she said. "When they visited their grandparents in Australia, they would ask Graham, 'When are we going home?' She and her surviving child, Esther, 14, never seriously considered leaving India," she said.

"I thought about leaving but then I think, 'What do I gain by going back?' I believe God brought me here. He will give me the strength to continue." She said she misses her family and "sometimes the pain is very deep," but, "I believe my husband and sons have gone to heaven. There is hope that this is not the end. I am going to see them again." Staines gets many encouraging letters from Hindus saying, "that what happened has nothing to do with Hinduism," she said.

She bears no ill will toward Dara Singh, the man police accuse of orchestrating the murders. "All of us deserve forgiveness. Christ forgave us—did any of us deserve forgiveness? He expects us to forgive others," she said. Police are offering rewards for information leading to the capture of Singh, who also is suspected in the murders of a Muslim merchant and Catholic priest, Arul Doss, *The Week* said.

religiontoday.crosswalk.com

Young warrior Does
Battle for D.C. Souls

"In order to stop youth violence, there are some things we will have to put down," Kelvin Wright told his audience. "We'll have to put down the guns and knives, put down the hatred and the backstabbing. And there are some things we'll have to pick up. We have to pick up love and unity and prayer."

Sound like preaching? You're right—but these are words from the mouth of a 16-year-old Washington, D.C. youth who was walking—correction: running—the devil's street life of drugs and drinking, stealing and lying, from age eleven. "I started smoking marijuana, drinking alcohol, and hanging out with my so-called friends. I wanted to be like them, because I wanted them to like me," he relates.

When his mother told him friends like that would only cause him to get locked up or killed, Kelvin began talking back to her and eventually ran away from home. "Doing things my way only made my troubles worse," Kelvin recalled. He eventually fell behind in school and was on the verge of dropping out altogether.

But one night "I was walking by this church, and I just felt convicted," Kelvin said. "Something said to me, 'Kelvin, you've got to stop living this way.'" The next day, he returned to the church for a Sunday service, and as the preacher spoke, "Something got a hold of me. I didn't understand what it was at the time. But I realize today that it was the Holy Spirit. Tears began to flow. I heard the preacher say that God can work it out, if you believe in your heart, and I just got up and cried even more. Before I knew it, I was shouting and doing a praise dance."

He was fourteen years old.

"I walked out of the church that day free at last, and my life would never be the same," the ninth-grader at H.R. Terrell Junior High in Washington recalled.

Kelvin has a knack for getting his peers to take a look at their own roles in creating their problems and to trust that the help they needed would be made available. Fear, hate, envy, glutton, whatever—the antidote to all of them, Kelvin explained, was faith.

Today, Kelvin has good news for both peers and parents: "Parents are the most important people in your lives," he says. "Parental pressure is greater than peer pressure. You have more influence than you know. Parents ought to be a child's parents and not a child's friend. It's about making sure that your child knows right from wrong."

Then he calls on parents to support their children, to congratulate them for doing well, as well as correcting them when they are wrong.

"Don't just give them money or buy them things," he said. "Hug them. Tell them you love them. That's what they really need."

Kelvin's classmates at Terrell named him the unofficial youth minister for their school. And he recently was appointed citywide president of the middle and junior high school student advisory council for D.C. public schools. He is also a youth minister at his church, Greater Rock Creek Baptist, where he preaches every fourth Sunday.

"Only God can defeat the enemy," Kelvin said. "The enemy comes into your life and plays you for a fool. I know. But God is good, all the time."

Courtland Milloy

Hot Water Bottle
on the Equator

Dr. Helen Roseveare, the famous British missionary doctor in Zaire, whose autobiography *Give Me This Mountain* is well worth reading, wrote about an event during her time in Africa. One evening, I was helping a mother give birth in the maternity ward. Despite our best efforts, she died, leaving us with a tiny premature baby and a crying two-year-old girl.

It would be hard to keep the baby alive, because we had neither electricity nor incubator, and the nights were often draughty and cool, even though we were on the equator. One student midwife went for the box we had for such babies and the cotton wool in which the baby would be wrapped. Another went to stoke up the fire and fill a hot water bottle. She came back shortly in distress to tell me that, in filling the bottle it had burst. Rubber perishes easily in the tropical climates.

"And it is our last hot water bottle!" she exclaimed.

As in the West, it is no good crying over spilled milk; so, in Central Africa, it might be considered no good crying over burst water bottles. They do not grow on trees and there are no drugstores down forest pathways.

"OK," I told her, "hold the baby as close to the fire as you can, and keep it out of draughts."

The following day, I had a prayer time with the orphans. I told them about the newly-born baby, the two-year-old orphan and the broken hot water bottle. During the prayer time, Ruth, a ten- year-old with the typical brutal directness of African children, prayed: please, God, send us a hot water bottle. Tomorrow will be too late, God, because the baby will be dead by then, so please send it this afternoon. I took a deep breath because of the prayer's directness, then heard her continue: and while you're at it, would you please send a doll for the little girl, so that she knows that you really love her?

To be honest, I could not believe that God would do that. Oh yes, God can do everything. I knew that, theoretically – it's written in the Bible. But there are limits, aren't there? I hadn't received any parcels from home for four years. And if anyone sent a parcel, why would they send a hot water bottle to tropical Africa?

Late in the afternoon, I heard that a car had come. By the time I arrived in my apartment, it had already left—but there was a large package on the veranda! I could feel tears welling up inside, and called the orphans so that we could open it together.

Apart from clothes, bandages and sultanas, the parcel contained—I could hardly believe my eyes!—a new rubber hot water bottle! I cried. I had not dared to ask God for it, but Ruth had! She had been sitting in the first row. She ran forward shouting, "If God sent the hot water bottle, he must have sent the doll, too!"

She dug to the bottom of the parcel and pulled out a beautiful small doll. Her eyes shone. She had not doubted for a moment. She looked up and asked, "Can we go to the little girl and give her the doll, so that she knows Jesus loves her?"

The parcel had been on the way for five months, sent

by a Sunday School class. The teacher had been so obedient to God that she even sent a hot water bottle to the equator. One of the girls had given a doll, five months before a ten-year-old African girl would pray "God, we need it this afternoon." The words in the Bible are true: "Before they call, I will answer them." (Isaiah 65:24)

Source: Dr. Helen Roseveare
Dawn Fridayfax

Prayers Help Restore
Son to Father

One day in May, missionary Travis Forsythe was driving home to Dabakala, Cote D'Ilvoire, where he and his wife serve among the Djimini people group. His 2-year-old son, Nathanael, was with him.

When Forsythe stopped for food late in the day at the city of Bouake, two bandits took the car from him at gunpoint. Forsythe clung to the open door of the vehicle, trying to convince the gunmen to let him get Nathanael out. The driver shot and wounded Forsythe, who chased the car as it sped away with his son in the back seat.

Forsythe's wife, Kim, and their 5-year-old daughter, Gloria, were not with him at the time. Kim Forsythe was observing her 30th birthday at home, ordered to bed by her doctor because of complications in her pregnancy.

By no coincidence whatever, the carjacking occurred on her birthday—a day when thousands of brothers and sisters in Christ back home were praying for her. The number of intercessors multiplied as word of the kidnapping almost immediately flashed through electronic prayer networks.

Forty-five minutes after the carjacking, the gunmen put Nathanael out of the vehicle and left him alone on a dark road in the village of Kaiola. Villagers put him in the care of a midwife, who fed and bathed the child and put him to bed while authorities located his parents. Nathanael was back with his father just hours after his abduction.

His father's injury was superficial, with the bullet miraculously passing through his right side between the ribs without hitting any vital organs. His mother, however, was hospitalized because the shock of the carjacking and kidnapping exacerbated the complications of her pregnancy.

"We never completely know what we are praying for when we pray for missionaries on the prayer calendar," said Wanda Lee, executive director of Woman's Missionary Union. "It's humbling and exhilarating when we learn about experiences like the Forsythes' and know, in faith, that our prayers played a role in resolving it."

"Praying for missionaries is the most important way we can help to support them," said Joanne Parker, editor of *Mission Mosaic*, WMU's magazine for women. "Missionaries are in a spiritual battle," she emphasized. "They can have all the money and training in the world, but that is still not going to empower them to accomplish the spiritual work of winning people to Christ. Our prayers undergird them in their spiritual work."

Baptist Press

Crisis At Wedgewood: Bringing Joy Out of Sorrow

(Editor's note: the following was relayed via email. The author is unknown, but the overall accuracy of the facts have been verified by Kari Fox, receptionist at Wedgewood Baptist Church in Fort Worth, Texas.)

On September 15, 1999 a gunman entered Wedgewood Baptist Church and killed seven people and injured seven others before taking his own life. What the media have not reported, however is how God has been so evident, both during and after the shooting. He has done amazing works!

Evidence of God's Control During the Shooting:
- ➤ The gunman fired over 100 bullets into a crowd of over 400, but only 14 people were hit.
- ➤ He did not shoot the more than 60 bullets he still had with him.
- ➤ The pipe bomb he threw did very little damage, as it exploded upward rather than outward. Most of the shrapnel landed in the balcony.
- ➤ One of the youths that was wounded (she was shielding a disabled friend with her body) has

scoliosis. The curvature in her spine apparently directed the bullet away from major organs, saving her from serious injury.

➤ One of the people in the church at the time was a paramedic, and he was able to stop the bleeding and stabilize injured people before the emergency crews arrived.

➤ Each children's worker stayed with his/her class even though they all had children elsewhere in the building, and some had teens in the sanctuary. Not one worker left his or her post.

➤ None of the adults who died had children.

➤ All seven victims were not just Christians, but bold Christians who were passionate about their faith. [*"You intended to harm, me, but God intended it for good to accomplish what is now being done, the saving of many lives"* (Gen. 50:20 NIV).]

What God Has Done Since the Shooting:

➤ Many denominations have pulled together to offer help and support. A church in Tulsa, Oklahoma, drove over five hours just so they could march around our church building and pray during our Sunday morning services.

➤ We have received over 13,000 emails, 20,000 cards, and $100,000 from all over the world. Al Meredith, our pastor has had the microphone in his face continually and has over and over given an outstanding answer to the reason for our hope. He presented the gospel beautifully on *Larry King Live* when prompted by a question by Vice President Al Gore.

➤ Because of the live news coverage and interviews, over 200 million people have heard the gospel because of this tragedy.

➤ At several schools, students met around their flagpoles the next day. At one school 25 students accepted Christ, 43 at another, and 110 at still another.

➤ Many members of Wedgwood Baptist Church are healing broken relationships within the body and experiencing spiritual renewal.

➤ Christian teachers all over North Texas have been able to share with their classes because the students are asking questions about their teachers' faith. One teacher led 22 students to Christ in her classroom.

➤ On the East Coast, where "See You at the Pole" was delayed because of the hurricane, record numbers of kids showed up to pray.

➤ CNN also broadcast the memorial services live. Amazingly, because one of the victim's families lives and works in Saudi Arabia, that country allowed the service to be broadcast there as well. In Saudi Arabia it is illegal to say the name of Jesus on the street.

➤ Because of that same CNN broadcast, 35 people in Japan gave their lives to Christ.

➤ A caller to an area Christian radio station said that he didn't know what those people had but he wanted it. The DJ proceeded to lead him to Christ. Many notes left in front of the church contain the same sentiment. Those who don't know Jesus want what we have!

These are just a few of the miracles that are happening. God's grace is almost overwhelming. Every time the gunman fired a bullet, he intended to take a life. Yet God turned that around and saved several lives for each bullet fired. The faith of those who died has been multiplied many times over.

"I thank my God through Jesus Christ for all of you, because your faith is being reported all over the world..." (Romans 1:8).

Pulpit Helps

Missing Grandma Found Alive in Car Atop Trees

Tillie Tooter is one tough grandma.

First, the 83-year-old Florida widow survived her Toyota Tercel's 32-foot drive off an interstate onto a dense growth of mangrove and willow trees.

Then, rescuers said, she endured three days of scorching heat and thunderstorms and three insect-infected nights in the confinement of her shattered car. Her cell phone, a ticket out of her predicament, lay just out of reach.

The rain, plentiful in South Florida at this time of year, and the fact that she was wearing her seat belt probably saved her life, said Dr. Moshe Stav, a Broward General Medical Center trauma surgeon.

Stav, who treated Tooter after she was rescued by Fort Lauderdale paramedics and firefighters Tuesday morning, said it was also her will to survive, despite a history of heart disease, high blood pressure and diabetes, that made the difference.

"The will to live, the will to fight are different in every person," Stav said. "Age itself is a minor factor, but not the only factor. She survived because she wanted to survive, because she was smart, and because she got a little bit of water."

She drank rainwater she collected in her steering-wheel cover and sucked on dew-soaked golf socks.

Finally, on Tuesday morning, rescuers used a fire truck ladder and a wire Stokes basket to lift a bruised and dehydrated—but fully conscious—Tooter out of her car and into a waiting ambulance.

Asked how the woman could have survived such an ordeal, Fort Lauderdale fire Lt. Michael Hicks said simply: "God."

Tooter made one last request of the sweating rescuers who rappelled over the highway wall, chain sawed a dozen trees to cut a path through the undergrowth, then used the Jaws of Life to cut the top off her silver 1995 Toyota: "Could you please get my pocketbook for me?"

"We were glad to oblige," said Fort Lauderdale Fire Division Chief Stephen McInerny. "This lady had it all together. That may have made a difference between surviving and dying."

Paramedics, escorted by Florida Highway Patrol troopers, took Tooter to Broward General Medical Center. She had bruises and insect bites but no broken bones, and was listed in serious condition. Doctors expect her to make a full recovery.

"I'm just so thankful and relieved she's alive," said a tearful Lori Simms, Tooter's granddaughter.

The case of the missing grandmother began at 2:54

a.m. EDT Saturday, when Tooter left her condominium in Pembroke Pines to pick up Simms and her boyfriend, Steven Poulos, at Fort Lauderdale-Hollywood International airport. Their flight from New Jersey had been delayed for several hours.

When she didn't show up at the airport, Simms called police.

For three days, officers searched canals, lakes and highways. There was no sign of Tillie Tooter until about 9 a.m. Tuesday, when a Department of Transportation worker collecting road debris along I-595 near the New River noticed something odd: A row of mangrove trees appeared to be bent over, as if a huge weight had crushed them.

The worker, Justin Vannelli, looked down to see what had happened.

"I saw the car first, then saw her legs sticking out," he said. "I told my dad to call an ambulance."

Justin's father, Chuck Vannelli, called 911.

'I see a lady.'

"It went over the top of the bridge wall," he told the dispatcher. "I see a lady down inside moving. The car went straight down."

Minutes later, Fort Lauderdale firefighters began to arrive.

"We put three medics over the wall immediately," McInerny said.

As a fleet of rescue vehicles arrived, police blocked off the interstate and traffic backed up for miles. Hicks' team found Tooter sprawled in the back seat, her legs propped over the steering wheel and stretched out over a crumpled front seat.

"She's conscious," he told his colleagues. "She's

talking to us, and this is the missing woman from Pembroke Pines."

They worked feverishly in the swamp below the highway, their boots sucked into the 8-inch deep ooze. Steam billowed from the standing water. Bugs were everywhere.

"This kind of thing, you don't have time to think about it," McInerny said. "It's got to be done."

As rescue workers labored to cut open the crumpled car, they kept Tooter talking.

"The first thing she said to me was, 'Can you get me out of here?'" said David Bourgouin, a firefighter/paramedic.

Florida Highway Patrol officials said the accident early Saturday happened when another vehicle struck Tooter's car.

"She was definitely struck by some vehicle in the left rear," said Lt. John Bagnardi, an FHP spokesman. "The back of her car had a lot of damage. There are so many scars and marks on the road and retaining wall that it's made it difficult to piece things together."

"She doesn't know if it was a truck or car, but that she was tagged in the rear."

The Toyota climbed the wall and rode it for 30 to 40 feet, Bagnardi said. It teetered for a moment, then tumbled over, landing on the driver's side.

"The trees cushioned the fall and her seat belt kept her from being thrown around," he said. "That's why she survived."

Hoping for a miracle

For the next three days, with thousands of cars and

trucks passing within feet of her car, Tooter hoped for a miracle. "Does anybody hear me? Please," she repeated, according to her granddaughter.

During her ordeal, Tooter wrote a goodbye note to her family, just in case. Family members would not share its contents.

When help arrived, Tooter told rescuers, "I'm very thirsty." She said she had slept very little. She was covered with ant and mosquito bites.

But McInerny said she was extremely sharp in responding to questions from medics trying to determine her condition.

"She knew her date of birth, her address and what flight her granddaughter was expected on," he said.

At a news conference on Tuesday afternoon, rescuers and family members praised Tooter's strength and courage. The steering wheel cover Tooter had used to collect water was still sticking out of Hicks' back pocket.

Hicks and his colleagues took a little over an hour to rescue Tooter. But they said she did the hardest work of all: she stayed alive.

"I personally have been at accidents where there were none of these obstacles, and it's taken longer," McInerny said. "This is one of the most dramatic rescues we've had since our department was founded in 1912."

Ardy Friedberg and Jeremy Milarsky
Sun-Sentinel Staff Writers Jodie Needle and Nancy McVicar contributed to this report.

A Modern Day Miracle

Insecurities reigned in downtown Port-Au-Prince, Haiti, everybody knew it was dangerous to be out in the streets after sundown. However, for Pastor Chavannes Jeune, it couldn't be helped. You see, Pastor Chavannes is one of the leading evangelists in the country, and he was preaching a revival. The service was over about 8:30 p.m., but he still needed to get across town to where he was staying with his in-laws.

He was alone as he started out in his double-cab Toyota. Suddenly he saw a little red Datsun in his rearview mirror. The guy must be nuts to drive that close. And now he was laying on the horn as though he wanted Pastor Chavannes to stop!

Finally the Datsun swerved and passed him. Then the crazy guy slammed on his brakes right in front of him, blocking the road. What could he do but stop!

A big burly guy dressed in shorts and a T-shirt jumped from the car. He came swaggering back with a big pistol clutched in his hand. Fortunately, the windows were rolled up. But he came to the driver's side and began hammering on the glass with the butt of the pistol! He must want him to roll it down. No way!

Now he was getting madder. Suddenly he turned the gun and started firing. Pastor Chavannes ducked down in the seat. He heard shots, one after another. There was the sound of glass breaking everywhere. Then it stopped and he looked up. There was the face again, now livid with rage. He could even see a gold cap on one of the assailant's front teeth! He was furious, and as though in slow motion, Pastor saw him turn and start back to his car for another weapon.

Pastor Chavannes saw his chance. He jammed the pickup into reverse, jumped the curb, and started around. But there was a big bus in the way. Plus he couldn't see because he had to keep his head down in case the guy had had time to get another gun. He did notice he almost ran the guy down as he went by.

The next thing he knew he was in the clear and driving down the street! He suddenly came to himself and had the distinct impression he needed to take over and start driving this vehicle! He pulled onto a side street and began to dodge from street to street, always looking back for the little red Datsun without a license plate. Finally a few minutes later he arrived at his father-in-laws' house.

Upstairs he was afraid to tell Marie Lucie what had happened. She was always worrying about him anyway. This would scare her to death. But he did tell his father-in-law. They decided to go down and see just how badly the vehicle had been damaged. When they got there, they couldn't find a scratch! Not a window was broken! There weren't even any bullet holes! It couldn't be! But there it was before their eyes.

The next day in broad daylight, Pastor Chavannes went back down that same street. Sure enough, there was the bus that had blocked his way. It hadn't been a dream after all. As he drove by, he looked more closely. Yes, there were bullet holes in the bus!

Two weeks later, there was a piece in the news about the insecurities in the country. They talked about people getting shot at night and about a certain pickup with the telephone company insignia on it and a little red Datsun without a license plate! Both vehicles had been involved in some of the crimes. In one case, a man had been shot thirteen times in the chest at close range!

But for Pastor Chavannes Jeune, for five special minutes, the left driver's side window had been bullet proof! God had spared the life of one of His most choice servants in Haiti.

Details have been checked with Pastor Jeune who vows for their authenticity. He has also authorized the publication of this account. Our prayer is that as others read it they will glorify God who is at work even today protecting His church and His people.

Paul Shingledecker

The Car Shouldn't Be Running

It was Sunday evening and my husband, Jim, and I had gone to church for an early meeting.

About fifteen minutes into the meeting, the phone rang. I went into the next room to answer it.

The woman on the other end of the line asked to speak with Rev. Pollard. I told her he was in a meeting and could not be disturbed.

"It's pretty important that I speak with him."

"I'm his wife. May I help you?"

She then told me she was Sandy, next-door neighbor to Jim's parents. "Mr. Pollard is dead. We believe he had a heart attack. We found him lying across the bed."

I stood there for a few minutes after I hung up, letting her words sink in. Tears welled up in my eyes. It was impossible to think of his being dead. He was such a wonderful, fun loving man. Why, just three months ago he'd been in Florida in our home! I remembered well the day he and Mrs. Pollard left Florida. It was June 27, my husband's birthday. No thought passed through my mind that day as I told them goodbye that this would be the last time I'd see him here on this earth.

I quickly wiped the tears from my eyes, whispered a prayer that God would be with us all and walked into the room where Jim was still conducting his meeting.

"Excuse me, but I need to see you in the other room," I said.

He walked into the room and I closed the door. "You'd better sit down."

"What's wrong?"

"I don't really know how to tell you this, but Sandy just called and told me your dad is dead. They think he had a heart attack."

I didn't know how he would take the news. He and his dad were very close. When we'd have a problem at the church, it was his dad to whom he would turn for advice. He'd call him and talk a long time. His dad usually had some wise counsel for him. I remembered once Jim jokingly said he talked to his dad rather than a psychiatrist.

Jim just looked at me and said, "Well, we know where he is. There's no doubt in my mind but that he is in Heaven right now."

He said he would preach that night. I was to go home and pack. We would leave immediately after church.

We had been having trouble with our car for some time. It had been missing and we had put off getting it fixed.

Jim put in a call to one of our deacons who owned a garage.

"Tony, I've just received word that my dad has died.

We have to leave immediately to go to Nashville. I hate to ask you to open your garage on Sunday, but could you please meet my son at the garage and check the car for me."

Barry, our son, took the car to Tony's.

When Barry came from Tony's, he said, "Tony said we should not put the car on the road. He said the accelerator coil was shot. He went on to say when the car quit, there would be no getting it started again until a new one was put on. If it did quit, it could be very difficult to find this part. It would probably have to be ordered from a dealer."

"Barry, go to church. As soon as church is over, tell your dad what Tony said."

Barry went to church. Soon both he and Jim were home.

"What are we going to do about the car?" I asked. I was thinking he would probably borrow one of the deacon's cars; thus his answer came as a surprise to me.

"We're going to pray over it, get in it, and go!"

"Well, okay," I said doubtfully, "if you think that's what we should do."

We did just that. We loaded the car, prayed and took off. The car missed two or three times just after we got on the interstate, but never again after that.

We left Hollywood, Florida and drove a straight seventeen hours to Nashville, Tennessee. The car never gave us any trouble!

The next day as we were going to the funeral home, the car began to miss again.

Jim looked at me and said, "That's my answer."

"What do you mean?"

"I told the Lord I needed to know if He had fixed it

149

permanently. I told Him if I needed to get it repaired before we went home to let it miss again."

A couple of days after the funeral, he took the car to the garage to be repaired. He told the mechanic what was wrong with it.

The mechanic got under the hood of the car and looked at the coil. After examining it, he looked at Jim with a strange look on his face. "Where did you say you came from?"

Jim explained how we had just driven from Hollywood, Florida a few days earlier.

An incredulous look came over the mechanics' face as he looked at him, shook his head and said, "I don't believe this. This coil is totally burned out. The car shouldn't be running!"

Jim shared with him the story of how his dad had died suddenly. Our mechanic had told him not to put the car on the road because the coil could go any time. He went on to tell him he was a minister and he had total faith in God to do anything.

"So, we just prayed over the car, got in it and drove nine hundred miles. We never had a minute's trouble. It never missed after the first couple of miles. I asked God to let me know if I should get it repaired before I drove back to Florida. The sign I needed to get it fixed would be if it started missing again. It did; and that's why I'm here. I know God got me here, but now He told me to get it repaired."

The mechanic looked at his friend who was standing nearby and said, "That's the second story like that that I have heard this week!"

Jeanetta Bearden Pollard

A VERY SPECIAL

CHRISTMAS

A young man who looked to be in his thirties told the following story on TV:

Mother had gone through a bad divorce. She had no money and Christmas was coming. She was troubled because she had nothing with which to buy presents for her children.

She went outside into the cold blustery air. She cried; she prayed. She stared up at the sky. The stars seemed to twinkle just for her. A sense of peace came over her; she knew what she would do.

About 2 am she went into the house and made hot chocolate. Then she woke the children. She told them she wanted them to get up, dress warmly and go outside to get their Christmas present. As they went outside, they noticed the snow had been swept from the first two steps. She asked them to sit down. She then served them hot chocolate and Christmas cookies.

She asked them to close their eyes and keep them closed until she counted to three.

When she gave them permission to open their eyes, she told them to look at the sky; to see all the beautiful, twinkling stars. She said this was their gift – all the beautiful stars. She told them the stars would always be with them even as she would always be with them. She told them this was a gift especially for them. No one else in the neighborhood was getting this gift.

The young man who was telling the story said he looked all around the neighborhood at all his friends' homes. All their houses were dark. It *was* true no one else was getting this gift of the twinkling stars.

Many Christmases had come and gone since this time, but none had surpassed this one. It was his favorite Christmas!

The moral of this story must be that it doesn't take money and material things to make a Christmas memory that will last through the ages.

James H. Pollard

OUTCAST

Stripped of dignity and hope, beaten and malnourished, the abandoned six-year-old lay on a mound of garbage to die. Then out of nowhere, a ray of sunshine enveloped her.

The city of Daejon was just waking up, still trying to forget the nightmare of the Korean War, when eight-year-old Stephanie slipped through the orphanage gate into the day's first light. Her skinny arms formed a circle around a bundle of smelly rags. As the oldest in the orphanage, it was her job to wash all the diapers. She walked two miles to the river, where she beat the diapers clean with a wide stick and sloshed them around in the icy water. By mid-afternoon, she was heading back to the orphanage to hang them up to dry.

It was hard work, but Stephanie didn't mind. Especially not today. Yesterday, the Swedish nurse, Iris Erickson told her: "Please help get all of the children ready. The foreigners are coming." On the way back to the orphanage, a string of kids followed Stephanie, shouting, as they always did, "Toogee! Toogee!" She didn't look at them, and walked on, her thoughts focused on all that had to be done at the orphanage.

Stephanie was used to people hassling her on the streets, and inside she believed that nasty word — toogee — was really her name, her true identity. In English it means foreign devil. "I thought I was the lowest you could get," says Stephanie. "That I was worse than a dog or pig and that my face was twisted and grotesque." But it was her curly hair and big, bright eyes that made people hate her. To the Koreans, she was "a child of foreigners"—a "devil" fathered by an American G. I. She was a reminder of everything they wanted to forget.

Hope for a Future

The orphanage chimes echoed throughout the compound. "I hope we didn't forget anything," Stephanie thought. She had spent hours scrubbing the babies, trying to make them as pretty as she could, even putting little ribbons in the girls' hair. "One of these babies is going to America," she said to herself, straining to hear the voices outside the gate. "And they're going to have a future."

The door squeaked open, and the worker motioned for the American couple to come in. Already they had been to six orphanages, looking for a little boy to call their own. They had already chosen a name for him, too: Stephen.

Fear and amazement gripped Stephanie's entire 30-pound body as she stared at the couple towering in the doorway. She had seen foreigners before—American soldiers and Miss Erickson, the blue-eyed nurse who took her off the streets into the orphanage almost two years ago. But these people now passing through the gate weren't like any Americans she knew before. "They were the tallest, roundest and strangest looking people I had ever seen," recalls Stephanie. Stephanie watched, fascinated as the huge man picked up a tiny baby and tucked it under his arm. Then she saw something else she had never seen in her life: tears trickling down a man's face. As she was trying to figure out why, Stephanie found herself edging closer to where he was. She stopped, frozen, when he looked at her with wet eyes.

He crouched in front of her and made noises with his lips she didn't understand as he spoke quietly to her in English. Her hair was more white than brown, teeming with lice. She was covered with boils and jagged scars. She had worms that sometimes crawled through her ears or her mouth. Her left eye rolled around lazily in its socket.

Now the man's massive hand was coming toward her face. It landed softly on her cheek and covered her like a smooth blanket. He stroked her, ever so gently. "My heart did a somersault." Stephanie remembers. "Inside I wanted to say, don't take that hand away, please love me." Instead, she yanked off the hand and spat on him.

A Dark Past

Before she came to live at the orphanage, when she was living on the streets, Stephanie determined that no matter what anyone did to her body, they would never hurt her on the inside. When some farmers tied her naked to a tree and let their children jab different parts of her body with sticks to see how she would respond to the pain, Stephanie learned not to cry. "You don't let people know that you hurt because the more you let them know that you hurt, the more pleasure it seems to give them," she explains. "By the time I was six I was dead emotionally."

Every since her mother abandoned her—Stephanie thinks she remembers her sending her away alone on a train when she was four—she had been running from village to village. She slept in caves, or under bridges and roasted locusts on rice straw or sucked the marrow from the bones the butchers threw out. Stephanie wanted to survive, and she kept hoping that her mommy or her daddy would be waiting somewhere for her. But many of the Korean villagers wanted to get rid of her. She was an ugly reminder of an ugly war.

A group of men once tied her to a waterwheel, hoping to drown her. Her mouth filled with mud and blood as she went round and round, thrashing and listening to the people laugh. Then, she heard a man's voice, deep and strong, telling them to stop. The man untied her and said to her, "Run, little girl, run. These people, they will hurt you." To this day she wonders if maybe he was an angel.

In the city, Stephanie became skilled at snatching food from the marketplace. But one time, because she was carrying a little girl she had found on the street, she was caught. "I remember being grabbed by a man and pulled back by my hair. And he said, 'It's that toogee again.' He recognized me somehow." Stephanie and the little girl were thrown over a wall into a bombed-out building that was infested with rats. "I held the little girl and rocked and screamed," Stephanie said. "I fainted, probably out of fear. I don't know how long I was out, but when I woke up, I saw with my six-year-old eyes how the rats had eaten away at that little girl." Miraculously, someone rescued Stephanie.

Soon after, Stephanie contracted cholera. "At seven years of age, I wanted to die," Stephanie recalls. "I knew what my future was, I hated myself and everything around me, especially the people. I didn't want to be abused anymore."

That's when in 1960, Iris Erickson found her laying on a garbage heap and brought her to live in the orphanage. Two years later, Americans David and Judy Merwin came to adopt a baby.

Home

"You're not going to believe this," David Merwin told his wife Judy on the way home from their visit to the orphanage, "but I have this feeling that we're supposed to adopt that little girl—the one who spit on me."

Judy Merwin laughed. She had that same stirring in her heart—and she felt it was from God. So the next day the Merwins returned to the orphanage and the little girl became their Stephanie.

Suddenly Stephanie had her own room and her own bed. And suddenly she had an identity. She was Stephanie Ann Merwin. And she was an American. Stephanie soon discovered that Americans like people who smile a lot. In a crowd of friends, she was always the bubbly one. As she grew older, she bleached her hair and talked her mom into buying her blue contacts, all so she would look more American. "But inside I didn't feel American or Korean, I was a dirty ugly toogee," Stephanie admits.

Stephanie's parents only knew the little about her past that the orphanage told them—just that she was found on the streets and that she was bi-racial. But the Merwins were troubled when they returned to Korea as missionaries after spending a year in the United States. Stephanie, at 12, always sat in the back of the church with her arms folded, and refused to speak to Korean people.

She wanted to forget her past at all cost. But her outer facade of happiness was wearing very thin during her late teens. She began pulling away from everyone in her life, and whenever she talked about herself, it was always negative. "I was full of bitterness and confusion and pain inside," says Stephanie. But she didn't want anybody to touch that, not her parents, and definitely not God.

One day her dad came up to her room, and sat at the end of the bed. He said, "I want to talk to you once more about Jesus." Stephanie remembered thinking: "Hey, I'm a walking encyclopedia when it comes to Jesus. I've been going to church most of my life, and I've been baptized. I don't need that anymore."

But Stephanie listened to her dad as he spoke gently to her. He talked about how when Jesus left heaven for earth, that he was conceived outside of marriage by a virgin. "He also asked if I'd thought about where Jesus was born," says Stephanie. "To me, the manger was just like the Christmas play every year. I didn't realize that it was a dark, dirty cave that never got cleaned out and that the only thing he had for a bed was a feeding trough." Stephanie's dad went on to explain how King Herod wanted to kill Jesus when he was a child because of what he represented, and how later on in life even his closest friends rejected him.

Stephanie began to cry as she realized how Jesus had been abused, and eventually even killed, so that He could identify with her. It was the first time she cried since she'd been thrown into the building with the rats. She prayed, opening up her life to God, asking Him to take her past, to forgive her sins and to make her whole.

That day was the beginning of a healing that's still happening in Stephanie's life. When she married her husband Darryl right out of high school, he knew she was adopted, but he didn't have an inkling of what her past really was. When Stephanie began to have nightmares, Darryl knew that they were more than just normal dreams. As Stephanie opened up to him they began to work through her past, and to pray together for God's help and healing.

Part of that healing has come since Stephanie began sharing her story publicly. She has a special concern for women, who often struggle with their sense of identity, and have been in abusive relationships. Stephanie is a regular speaker for women's groups and has traveled across the world to tell her story, even to Korea.

As she talks about her life, Stephanie still marvels that she survived those childhood dangers and realizes how fortunate she is to be alive and doing what she's doing today. "You know, it was amazing, but every time I was in trouble, there was always someone who rescued me," Stephanie recalls. "And each time the person would tell me, 'Little girl, you must live.' I don't know if they were angels or just people God used, but I do know that God spared my life. He never gave up on me. And I've learned He never will."

What about you? Do you bear scars that will not heal? Is your past making it difficult to see God's future for you?

God wants to be our leverage in living, empowering us to feel better about ourselves, more excited about our future, more grateful for those we love and more enthusiastic about our faith.

Ask God to be the leverage you need in being more confident in who you are, more in tune with those you love, and more effective in your marketplace. Why not pray this simple prayer and by faith invite Him to fill you with His spirit:

> Dear Father, I need you. I acknowledge that I have sinned against you by directing my own life. I thank You that You have forgiven my sins through Christ's death on the cross for me. I now invite Christ to again take His place on the throne

of my life. Fill me with the Holy Spirit as You commanded me to be filled, and as You promised in Your word that You would do if I asked in faith. I pray this in the name of Jesus. As an expression of my faith, I thank You for directing my life and for filling me with the Holy Spirit. Amen."

Stacy Wiebe

SELECTED BIBLIOGRAPHY

Tell Them for Me by John Powell. Reprinted by permission of the author.

Drawn by God from *God Owns My Business* by Stanley Tam. Copyright ©1969 by Stanley Tam. Reprinted by permission of Stanley Tam.

The Promise of God by Betty Swinford. If anyone can provide knowledge of the original source of this story or surviving heir, please relay this information to Jeanetta B. Pollard, PO Box 7, Boaz, Ky. 42027.

Electrifying Experience by Brian Cribb. Reprinted by permission of Baptist Press.

From Triumph to Tragedy by Darlene M. Mazzone from Paducah Patriot 2000 edition of *Paducah Life Magazine*. Reprinted by permission of the author.

When Does God Pick Flowers by Bruce Hawthorne from the Christian Brotherhood News Letter. Reprinted by permission of the author.

Columbine Killers Mock Christ. Reprinted by permission of Religion Today (http://news.crosswalk.com/religion).

Miracles Set Course for "God's Navy" by Norise Jastillana and Sandy Van. Reprinted by permission of the author.

Where Healing Begins by Bud Welch. Reprinted with permission from *Guideposts* ©1999 by Guideposts, Carmel, N.Y. 10512.

161

of Religion Today (http://news.crosswalk.com/religion).

God Answers Prayer by Vickie Bailey. Reprinted by permission of the author.

Martyr's Widow Carries On. Reprinted by permission of Religion Today (http://news.crosswalk.com/religion).

Young Warrior Does Battle for D.C. Souls. ©2000, The Washington Post. Reprinted with permission.

Hot Water Bottle on the Equator from Dawn Fridayfax. Text © Dawn Europa. Web pages copyright © 1996 Jesus Fellowship Church.

Prayer Helps Restore Son to Father. Reprinted by permission of Religion Today (http://news.crosswalk.com/Religion).

Crisis at Wedgwood from Pulpit Helps. Reprinted with permission by the editor.

Missing Grandma Found Alive in Car Atop Trees. Reprinted with permission from the South Florida Sun-Sentinel.

A Modern Day Miracle. Reprinted by permission from the World Gospel Mission Publishing Department.

The Outcast. Reprinted with permission from Christian Women Today.com. http://www.christianwomentoday.com

Editor's After Word

I am always interested in stories that tell the remarkable things God is doing in people's lives today. If you would like to share your story with me, please send it to Jeanetta Pollard at P. O. Box 7, Boaz, Kentucky 42027.

Also if you have a wedding or Christmas story that is unusual, touching or amusing, I would be interested in seeing these. Please send them to me at the address listed above.

If you would like to order a copy of this book, you may contact me at this address or email me at Success@apex.net, or phone me at 270-851-7699, or visit my website at www.jeanettapollard.com.

Jeanetta Bearden Pollard